A CREATIVE GUIDE TO

PAINTING
ON SILK

A CREATIVE GUIDE TO

PAINTING
ON SILK

ANGELIKA ORTHAUS

PHOTOGRAPHY BY
JURGEN ORTHAUS

First published in the UK in 1994 by
New Holland (Publishers) Ltd
37 Connaught Street, London W2 2AZ

First published as *Seidenmalerei* in 1991 by Mosaik Verlag GmbH, Munich

English translation copyright © 1994 New Holland (Publishers) Ltd
Copyright © 1994 Mosaik Verlag GmbH, Munich

ISBN 1 85368 345 0

Editor: Coral Walker
Technical consultants: Alan Hebden and Sarbjitt Natt
Photographer: Jürgen Orthaus
Cover design: Chris Dymond

Typeset by Dorwyn Ltd, Rowlands Castle, Hants
Reproduction by Filmsatz Schröter, Munich
Printed and bound in Singapore by Tien Wah Press (Pte.) Ltd

CONTENTS

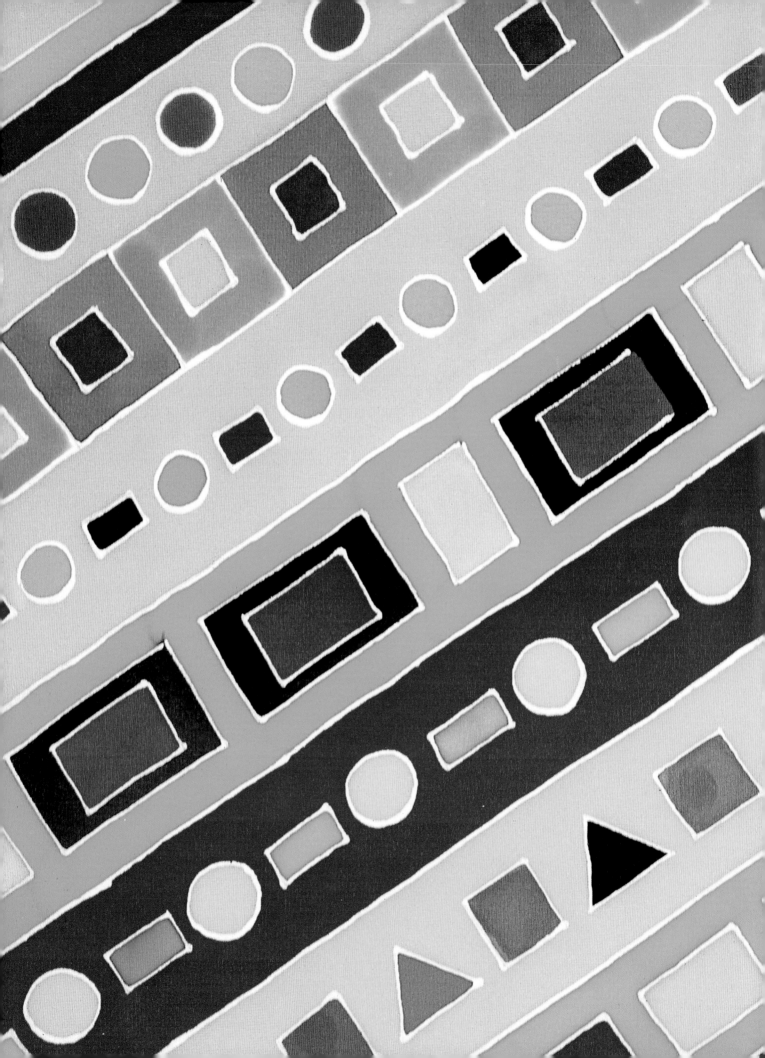

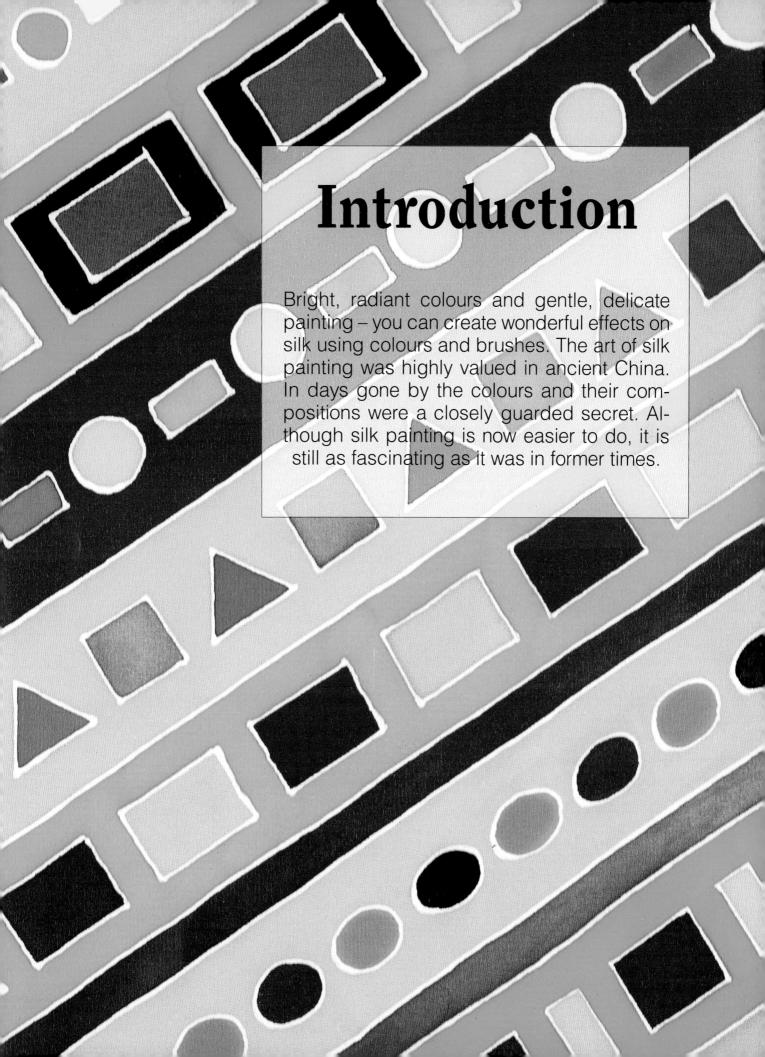

Introduction

Bright, radiant colours and gentle, delicate painting – you can create wonderful effects on silk using colours and brushes. The art of silk painting was highly valued in ancient China. In days gone by the colours and their compositions were a closely guarded secret. Although silk painting is now easier to do, it is still as fascinating as it was in former times.

SILK PAINTING FOR EVERYONE

This book provides a readily understandable entry into the wonderful world of silk painting. You need no specialist knowledge. Everything will be clearly explained, from the materials and the painting techniques to creating the actual pictures. This makes the painting very easy because at almost every stage, you can compare your own designs with the examples given in this book. Even if you already have some experience of silk painting, this book will give you many new ideas because it explains not only the techniques but also many of the rules governing design and composition.

Before you begin painting, be sure to read the chapter entitled 'Working Materials' (page 10). This tells you not only what you need to be able to paint, but also what to do with the materials. It covers selecting and stretching silk; how to work with colours and outliners; and fixing.

In the chapter 'Painting on Silk' (page 30) the different silk painting techniques are explained.

Of course, every piece of silk painting varies. In the main it would be impossible to make exact copies of the pictures in this book; indeed,

this is not what is required because your paintings should reflect your own personal style. You will, however, be able to use the step-by-step painting instructions to see if you are achieving the same effects in your pictures as in the examples given in this book.

With each picture, details are given of which techniques to apply and which materials and colours you require.

The colour names refer to those used by the Deka company. You can of course use colours provided by other manufacturers.

Once you have read this chapter and tried out the various techniques, you will be well versed in the basics of silk painting.

The chapter 'The World of Colours' (page 84) trains you in the use of colour. You will learn, for example, how to mix colours to create new shades, and from this will be able to put together your own personal colour palette. Of course, you will also learn how best to combine certain colours so as to enhance

the effect of the individual colours.

In the last two chapters, 'Creating Designs' (page 98) and 'Design Ideas' (page 116), you will find not only a large number of pictures with very precise painting instructions, but also helpful advice and a great many practical tips which you can try out for yourself using the illustrated examples.

1 Shapes and colours
Clear lines, beautiful colour merging. Outliners, overlaying and watercolour techniques go well together.

2 Small tree in wood
This picture is drawn freehand using a paintbrush.

3 Playing with colours
The use of the overlaying technique opens up fascinating possibilities.

1

2

An amazing diversity – the techniques

At the outset, the many new technical terms may seem a little confusing. The reason for this is that silk painting offers a great many creative possibilities. You can paint on silk just as if you were painting with watercolours – in other words, you can paint the colours directly on to wet silk. This creates very attractive colour runs. So in silk painting, too, this technique is known as the **watercolour technique**. If colour thinners are applied, the term used is the **thinning technique**. If colours are painted into one another on wet silk, this is known as the **wet-on-wet technique**.

Silk painting also allows another very special technique, over and above those mentioned above, which prevents colours running: painting with outliners. Where an outliner has been applied to silk, colours can no longer penetrate the material. Using the **outliner technique** you can paint very clearly defined areas of colour, giving a graphic effect. A further development in and variation on the outliner technique is the **overlaying technique**.

You can also influence the colours by using the **salt technique**. This results in flower-like and crystal-shaped structures.

Silk painting – in brief

Before you begin painting, test to see if the silk takes up the colour. If not, wash the silk (see page 13).

Draw a preliminary sketch using a soft pencil (3B) or, preferably, an 'Auto Fade Pen' on to the silk (see page 32).

Before it can be painted, the silk is stretched across a frame. It must not sag and there should be no stretch lines (see page 22).

Once painting is completed, the silk painting must be fixed so that the colours do not change with time. Steam or an electric iron is used for the fixing process, depending on the type of silk painting colour employed (see page 26).

After fixing, clear outliner is removed, either by specialist dry cleaning or by washing, depending on the product (see page 18). Surplus colour must be washed out of items of clothing (see page 27).

3

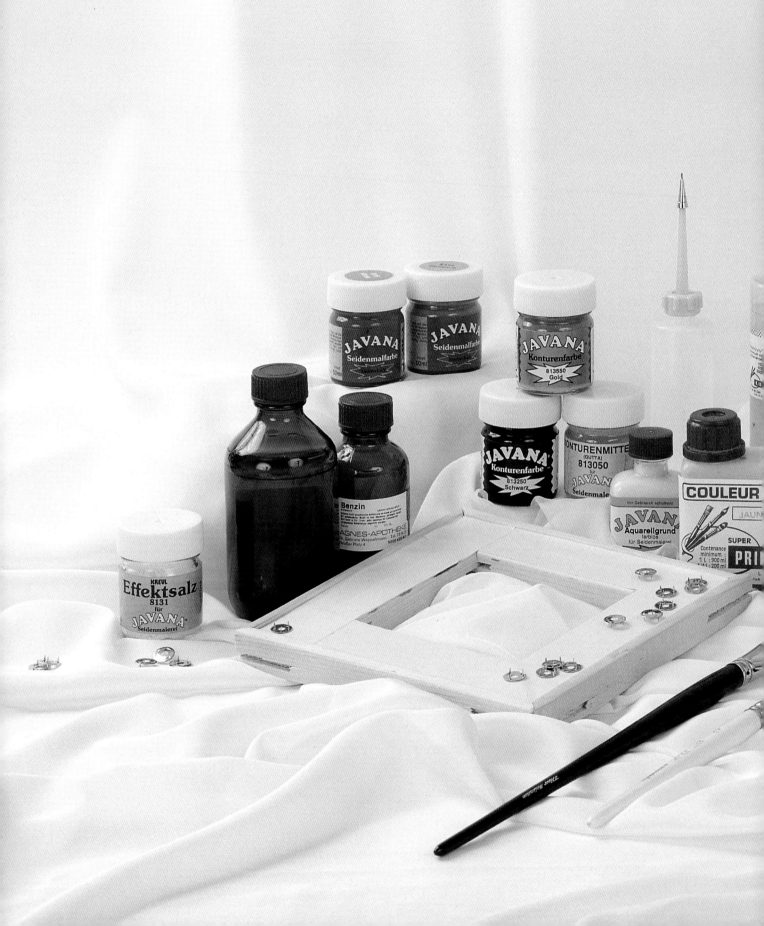

Working materials

You do not need many tools for silk painting: a few colours, thinners, outliners, brushes, pins, silk and a stretching frame. The range of silk painting products on offer continues to grow, however, making selection more difficult. So in this chapter you will be given an overview of the most important materials and the ways in which they can be used.

SILK

Every piece of silk is different

The drop test is a good way of assessing the quality of a piece of silk as a surface for silk painting. Dab a little colour on to the silk. The result can be seen instantly. On thin silk the colour will spread out well and thus painting areas of even colour will be straightforward. The colours are light. On heavy silk the colours are more intense but they do not flow as well. The examples in this book were painted on habutai (medium to heavy) silk nos 8 and 10 and on crêpe de Chine 56–58g. These silks are particularly well suited to silk painting.

Habutai silks, medium weight (no. 8 32–34g/1oz and no. 10 42–44g/1¼oz), are ideal for beginners. Thanks to the good spreading properties of the colours, all the painting techniques can easily be carried out on this silk. Furthermore, habutai silk is very reasonably priced. It is a smooth silk used for many different applications. Depending on the weight, it can be used, for example, for scarves, blouses or cushions. It is available in various weights from no 0.5 (= 20–22g/¾oz) to no 014 (= 66–68g/2oz).

Crêpe de Chine has a somewhat more grainy feel. It should not be too crêped. Its surface has a gentle shine. Crêpe de Chine is very soft to the touch and, in view of its crease-proof property, is recommended for use in the fashion and home sectors. Before painting on crêpe de Chine, use habutai silk to see how colours and silk react with one another. If you already have some experience of silk painting, crêpe de Chine is an excellent painting surface. Some shrinkage may be experienced if crêpe de Chine is steam-fixed.

Twill, too, is a good painting surface. Twill is a thick, shiny, supple, economical silk suitable for shawls, cushions and scarves.

Thin and medium-heavy silks make very attractive garments owing to their soft hang. It should be borne in mind, however, that thin silks are very delicate and have a tendency to snag easily.

Colours on shimmering silk

The soft shine of silk and its fine texture lend silk painting a special effect. On silk, colours become particularly intense. There are many different qualities of silk available: smooth- or rough-surfaced silk; thin and delicate or with a heavy drape; transparent or thickly woven.

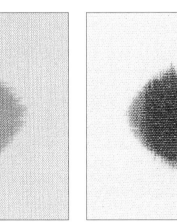

1

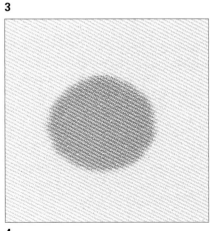

3

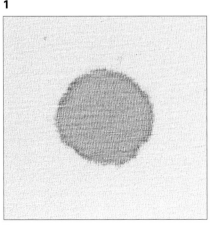

2

4

1 Green spot on thin habutai silk. The colour spreads well.

2 Red spot on a fine pure silk chiffon. Here, too, the colour spreads quickly. The effect is that of a very light colour.

3 Reddish-purple spot on a heavy-quality crêpe de Chine. The colour is intense but it runs very little.

4 Yellow spot on raw silk twill. The colour hardly runs at all and stands out well.

So before you begin painting, think about how you want to paint on the silk and what you want to use the finished work for later.

Thin silk is easy to paint because it allows the colours to spread easily. Outliners, too, penetrate light cloth particularly well. Habutai silk, twill, crêpe de Chine and chiffon are all well suited to the outliner technique. For best results, thick, heavy silks such as bourette or wild silk (tussah silk, honan, doupion), which also have an uneven woven surface, should be painted wet-on-wet using the watercolour technique. Using this free-painting method the silk's surface structure can be integrated.

Preparing the silk

Before you begin painting, test to see if the silk takes up the colours well. Most fabrics like silks have a manufactured finish, which stops the colours penetrating the silk. It must be washed out using a mild washing agent at a maximum of 40°C (104°F).

You can obtain pure silk that has not been treated in any way from silk painting supply shops.

Different silks will vary in the degree to which they shrink. They should therefore be pre-washed before cutting.

1 Pure silk taffeta
2 China habutai, pure white, approx 20 g/½ oz
3 Bourette, natural
4 Honan Best, select, natural
5 Bourette, satin, natural
6 Organza, dyed
7 Crêpe de Chine, dyed, approx 100 g/ 3 oz

COLOURS

A large selection

Silk painting colours are very strong. The liquid concentrates penetrate the silk to such an extent that the painting is of equal quality on both sides of the material. The colours are transparent, so that painted silk also has a very attractive appearance even in counter-light. You can read about how to thin colours and what effect this has on the colours' properties in the section entitled 'Thinning Techniques' (page 70).

Basically you have a choice of three different types of colour.

Traditional silk painting colours

These are strong, bright colours. They are thinned using commercially available thinner, or a mixture of alcohol and water, or pure water. They dissolve completely in the liquid and thoroughly penetrate the silk without leaving any residue. Spirit-based outliner is used with these colours.

Traditional silk painting colours are fixed using steam. Due to their excellent painting properties and their brilliant colour effect, these traditional silk painting colours are preferred by professionals.

Products: Deka Dupont, Sennelier (Tinfix and Super Tinfix), Serticolor, Elbesoie, Princecolor.

Iron-fixable silk painting colours

These colours are thinned using water. The outliner used with iron-fixable colours is water-soluble, and may therefore partially dissolve in the water used to thin the colours when painting. For this reason, water-soluble outliners are not suitable for the overlaying technique (see page 50). Colour penetration is good. The advantage with these colours is that they can very easily be fixed using an iron.

1

2

3

Products: Deka-Silk, Elbetex, Javana, Marabu-Silk.

Liquid-fixable colours
These colours are fixed using a chemical liquid. They were not used for the examples in this book.

Colour mixing
You can mix together colours produced by different manufacturers. I have done this with steam-fixable colours which I have often used together in one picture. You can also use steam-fixable and iron-fixable colours together provided you use spirit-based outliner, such as gutta, and then fix the painting using steam. Steam increases the intensity of all types of colours.

All the paintings in this book were carried out using Deka silk painting colours. The colour charts showing the colour names for each picture refer to Deka colours. Using the colour charts it is easy to select colours produced by other manufacturers or to mix together colour tones yourself.

In the first instance the basic primary colours red, yellow and blue will suffice. You can use these basic colours to mix up all the other colours

(see 'The World of Colours' on page 84). Buy your favourite colours ready mixed; this will ensure that the colour tones are always the same.

Always follow the manufacturer's instructions carefully. Never leave the colour bottles open after use. Pour original colours back into the bottles from which they came. If unused or mixed, store colour in closed jars or bottles. Any colour residue should immediately be washed off the mixing palette.

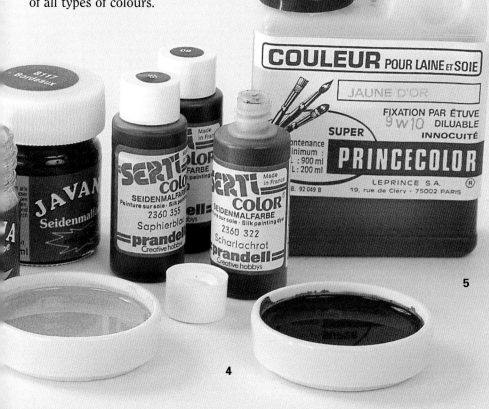

Choice of colours, from left to right:
1 Deka-Silk, iron-fixable colour
2 Deka, steam-fixable colour
3 Javana, iron-fixable colour
4 Serticolor, steam-fixable colour
5 Princecolor, steam-fixable colour

BRUSHES

Only the best is good enough

The paintbrushes are as important as the colours and silk on which you are painting. In the beginning you would do better to buy one expensive, good-quality brush than several cheaper brushes; you really will not regret it.

Cheap brushes do not hold the colour well and soon become tatty to the extent that you are not able to continue serious painting with them. The hair quality and the shape of the brush are both important.

A **round brush** when wet would have a tapered, delicately slender tip.

A **flat brush** should retain its right-angular shape, even during paint-ing. Its front should curve gently inwards.

The best and most expensive brushes are **sable brushes**. They retain colour very well and release it evenly so that when painting you are not taken by surprise with a sudden release of colour. Also, using a sable brush you can paint large areas in one stroke without having to dip the brush into the colour. The elasticity of sable allows you to work using free, light brush strokes. Painting with these brushes is a lot of fun. They react very sensitively to your personal painting method, your stroke and the pressure you apply to the brush.

Sable brushes do not have to be expensive. Less expensive versions are available; these are mixtures of sable and other animal hair or fibres.

Squirrel hair brushes are very good value for money.

Chinese and Japanese brushes are also suitable for silk painting.

When choosing your brushes you will need to bear in mind what it is you want to paint, ie large or small areas, or fine detail. The painting techniques also need to be taken into account.

To begin with a round brush no 8 or 9 made of sable will suffice. These brushes will enable you to paint smaller areas, and you can use the tip to paint fine lines.

A no 3 sable brush is particularly suited to painting fine detail. It is also practical to have an additional brush, a no 12 squirrel hair brush, for example, for painting larger areas and for washing out the colours with water. You will need a silk

1   2   3   4   5   6

paint brush no 30 or 40 for painting large areas on scarves and shawls.

Brushes are delicate, sensitive objects. They must therefore be treated with care. Brushes should never stand on their hairs. This causes them to lose their shape and eventually they become unusable and have to be replaced. Always ensure that brushes are well washed after painting. Using a rapid hand movement, shake out the brush so that it regains its original shape. When not in use, place the brush upright, with the tip facing upwards, in a jar or other container. To protect delicate brush tips it is advisable to place a thin plastic cover over them and down the shaft. Good brushes are usually supplied with such a protective sheath, so keep any you buy for this purpose.

Brush collection, from left to right

1 Sable brush no 9
2 Silk painting brush no 14
3 Silk painting brush no 8, flat/pointed
4 Silk painting brush no 40, for large areas
5 Silk painting brush no 6
6 Toray hair brush, gold sable no 4
7 Toray hair brush, gold sable no 6
8 Silk painting brush no 8
9 Sable brush no 3
10 Toray hair fan brush
11 Red sable brush no 6
12 Toray hair brush, gold sable no 8
13 Red sable brush no 8
14 Flat sable brush no 18

7   8   9   10   11   12   13   14

OUTLINERS

Creating contours

You can paint sharp contours and clearly defined areas of colour on silk using outliners. They are relatively viscous and do not run, thus enabling you to draw very precise lines. Where an outliner has been applied the colour will not be able to penetrate the fabric. The area of colour is therefore defined by the outliner.

Colourless outliners leave the silk as it is. In other words, a colourless outliner will leave unpainted silk white, and silk that has already been painted – the colour it was painted. You can also paint with coloured outliners.

For application purposes, the outliner is placed in a pipette bottle at the tip of which there is a nib attachment. This attachment allows you to draw fine lines.

At the outset you will need a pipette bottle with a metal nib and a colourless outliner.

You will find detailed instructions on working with outliners in the section entitled 'Outliner Techniques' (page 36).

There are two different types of outliner available, both of which have their own advantages and disadvantages. There are the water-soluble outliners; and spirit-based outliners generally known as gutta. The silk paintings in this book were produced using both types of outliner.

Water soluble outliners

As their name suggests, these can be thinned using water, although most are ready for use and need not be diluted. Water-soluble outliners are used in conjunction with iron-fixable colours. Manufacturers offer iron-fixable colours that coordinate well with water-soluble outliners. Their advantage is that they are simple and easy to process. You do not need any complicated equipment to fix them; in fact, all you need is an iron. In the case of coloured outliners, the outliner colour is fixed at the same time as the silk paint colours and thus remains fixed in the material. Colourless outliners are simply washed out using luke-warm water. This should be done as soon

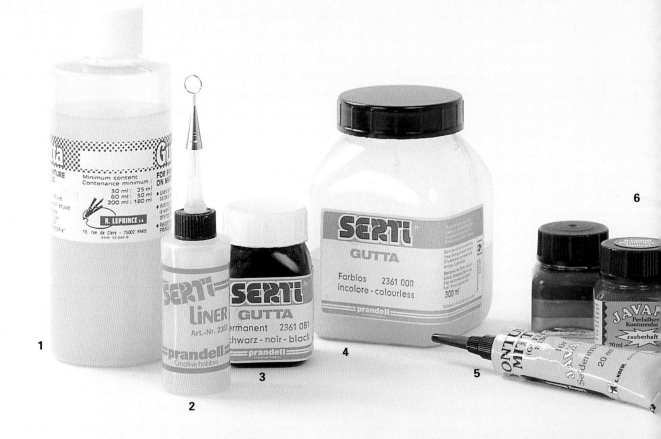

as possible after fixing, because in time the outliner hardens and cannot then later be completely removed.

If you add a lot of water to your colours your outliner may dissolve slightly and thus have gaps in it. As a result the colours may bleed through the outliners. To avoid this you should allow the outliner to dry thoroughly before painting with colours. Water-soluble outliners are not suitable when using the overlaying technique.

Spirit-based outliners

Spirit-based outliner, also known as gutta, is a traditional silk painting agent.

'Essence F' is well suited to thinning spirit-based outliner. The outlines must be completely dry before painting begins or they will not retain the colour. After it has been fixed using steam, the spirit-based outliner can be removed by dry cleaning, or by immersing the silk in a regular petrol bath or in white spirit, then washing in soapy water.

Overall, the after-treatment – which involves steam fixing and cleaning – requires considerably greater time and money than when working with water-soluble materials. The advantage of spirit-based outliner over water-soluble outliner is the former's low sensitivity to colours that have undergone considerable thinning. Therefore spirit-based outliner is a good agent to use when employing the overlaying technique (see page 50).

For each of the illustrated examples shown in this book, details are given as to which outliner was used. Pictures marked 'spirit-based outliner' must be painted using this substance. Designs simply marked 'outliner' can be painted using either type and the appropriate silk painting colour. This is true of most of the examples. The pictures in this book have been painted using Deka water-soluble outliners and Serti spirit-based outliners.

Colourless and coloured outliners, from left to right:
1 Spirit-based outliner by Princecolor
2 Spirit-based outliner by Serticolor, decanted into a pipette bottle
3 Black Serti spirit-based outliner, permanent
4 Colourless Serti spirit-based outliner
5 Colourless Javana water-soluble outliner in a tube
6 Javana Pearl-Silver water-soluble coloured outliners in blue, bright red and red
7 Two Deka pipette bottles with nib and colourless and pink water-soluble outliner
8 Colourless Javana water-soluble outliner
9 Javana pipette bottle with nib
10 Colourless Deka water-soluble outliner
11 Deka water-soluble outliner in gold and silver

NIBS AND PIPETTES

For painting purposes outliners are poured into small pipette bottles.

These plastic pipette bottles have a long tip which is screwed on to the top of the bottle. Then, in order to be able to paint, a hollow metal needle – the nib attachment – is inserted or screwed on to this.

Preparation
Before you can use the pipette bottle you have to pierce a hole in the top of the tip through which the outliner can flow. If the hole is not large enough, take a knife and cut off a small section from the tip.

Before you begin, unscrew the tip from the bottle, pour the outliner into the bottle and then screw the tip back on again. Insert or screw the nib attachment into the nib. You will then be able to use it to draw very fine and precise outlines.

Nib attachments
Nibs are available in various line widths. The most common are 0.5 mm, 0.6 mm and 0.8 mm. If, when drawing, you feel that the nib is not attached securely enough, use a little masking tape to prevent it from slipping.

If you wish to use various line widths in your painting, prepare the appropriate number of pipette bottles fitted with the relevant nibs and filled with outliner. This will enable you to work quickly. Make sure that the outliner is thinned to suit the width of the nib, thereby ensuring a good flow.

The nib comes complete with a

1

2

3

4

small wire. This is inserted into the nib when you are not painting to prevent it becoming blocked. You can also use the wire to unblock nib attachments. If you intend not to paint for some time, remove the nib and seal off the tip of the pipette bottle with a plastic cap. This will prevent the solution from thickening or evaporating. Better still, pour the outliner back into its original bottle. If the outliner has thickened, use the appropriate dilutant to thin it once again.

Cleaning and storing

Clean the pipette bottle and nib according to the type of outliner used, ie for spirit-based outliner use Essence F, and for water-soluble outliner use water.

If you are working with spirit-based outliner you can leave the pipette bottles full and store them in a jar with Essence F. Remove the nibs from the bottles and store them in a jar also with Essence F. Close the jars securely when you have finished.

Working with outliners, from left to right:
1 Pipette bottle in its original state
2 Pipette bottle filled with outliner and closed using a plastic cap
3 Pipette bottle with nib attachment ready for painting
4 Metal nibs
5 Two jars containing Essence F, used for storing nibs and pipette bottles

FRAMES

Practical systems

For painting purposes, the silk needs to be stretched as tightly as possible across a frame. You can either make the frame yourself out of strips of soft wood, or you can buy a ready-made frame. Check to see that the edges of the frame form an even surface, ie they should not lie one on top of the other. This will ensure that the silk can be stretched smoothly.

The three frame systems shown below have proved very reliable. The silk can be stretched flat across them. The choice of frame will depend on the size of the piece of silk to be painted. To begin with a 50 × 50 cm (20 × 20 in) wooden slat frame should be sufficient. You may, however, also like to purchase a few cheap wedge frame slats in 30 cm, 40 cm and 50 cm (12 in, 16 in and 20 in) lengths.

For scarves you will need a frame with sides at least 1 metre (3 ft 4 in) long. You should bear in mind that the ends of the slats on adjustable frames jut out at the corners if the frame is not being used to its full size. If they protrude too far, they can obstruct you during your work.

Adjustable sliding frame
This is a very convenient solution. The frame comprises four wooden slats of wood with slits and pegs that can be slotted into one another. This means the frame can be adjusted to any size.

Sliding frames are available in various sizes.

Adjustable wooden slat frame
This comprises four wooden slats out of which grooves have been sawn, 4 or 5 cm (1¾–2 in) apart. This frame can therefore be used to produce many different formats.

This is a cheap and practical frame system available commercially in several sizes.

Wedge frame
Wedge frames are used in oil painting to stretch the canvas.

They are equally well suited to silk painting, as wedge frame slats are available in many different lengths from 15 cm (6 in) upwards. They are available from artist's suppliers. The slats can be bought separately, thus enabling you to create elongated formats.

To make a frame you need four slats which are placed together at right angles and then gently hammered together using a small hammer. Do not hammer the frame together too tightly as this will cause the wood to split.

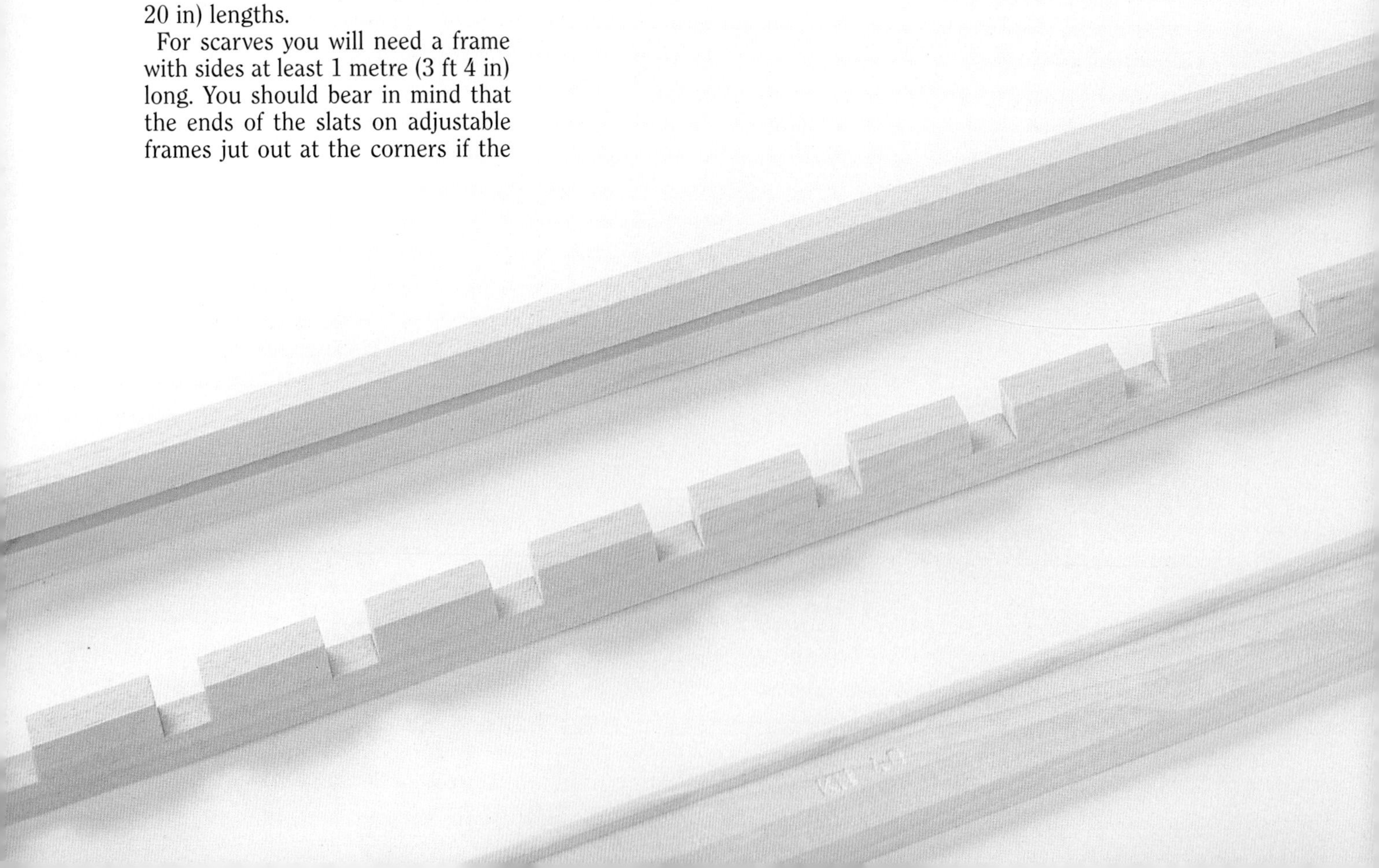

The frames can easily be taken apart again and put together in different formats.

Making your own frames

If the shape you require is unusual, you can easily make your own frame. Do not use wood that is too hard as this could cause problems when pressing in the three-point pins used to secure the silk. Screw the slats together at the corners, making sure that all protrusions face inwards or downwards so that there is a flat surface on the top across which the silk will be stretched.

Lay large frames on painting trestles when it comes to the painting stage. This allows the silk to be suspended freely without the risk of it coming into contact with work surfaces or something similar. Ensure that the frame does not slip by securing it on to the trestles using adhesive tape or clamps.

Three proven frame systems:

Top: Adjustable sliding frame
Middle: Adjustable wooden slot frame
Bottom: Wedge-frame slats

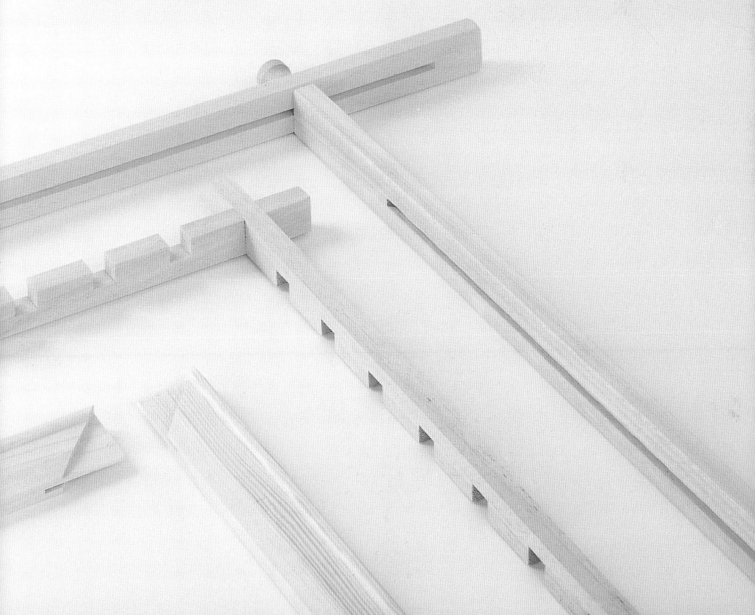

STRETCHING SILK

Stretching is the key

The more evenly and tightly the silk is stretched across the frame, the easier it is to paint. Before painting begins, the frame should be covered with masking tape so that no colour can penetrate the wood. This colour could stain any silk that you stretch across the frame at a later stage and thus spoil your painting. There is a particular danger of this happening when you are painting wet-on-wet.

Use a flat paper masking tape to stick the silk down. This must be replaced for each new painting. Flat vinyl adhesive tape can simply be wiped with a damp cloth after painting to remove the colour.

Once you have transferred the design to the silk (see page 32), stretch the silk across the frame. Remember that you should not use those parts of the silk that lie on the actual frame for your design. Therefore, when cutting the silk, allow for a border and use only the surface within the frame for your design.

To stretch the silk across the frame you can use push-pins or, better still, three-point architects' pins. Normal drawing pins are not advisable as they leave large holes in the silk and can cause the silk to tear. By contrast, three-point pins have hardly any effect on the silk.

The first thing you should do is firmly pin down the silk at the four corners. Then fix one side using three-point pins. It is better to place the pins close together rather than too far apart. A distance of between 3–6 cm (1¼–2¼ in) is recommended.

Next fix down the opposite side firmly. Make sure that the pins are not inserted immediately opposite those on the first side as this could create a stretch line.

Ensure that the silk is stretched as tight as a drum across the frame. Under no circumstances should the silk sag, as this could cause colour to collect in some areas.

As you paint the silk, the dampness may cause it to stretch. If this happens, the silk must be re-stretched across the frame. This is easily done if you are using an adjustable sliding frame. You simply loosen the fixing devices and then extend the frame accordingly. With all other types of frame the pins must be removed. In most cases, all you will need to do is re-stretch one side of the silk. To do this, remove one pin, stretch the silk and replace the pin; then continue

in the same fashion with the other pins.

Make sure that when you are painting, any stretching or movement of the silk within the frame does not cause it to come into contact with any other surface.

The silk should never come into contact with your work table as this may cause spots to appear. If adequate stretching of larger pieces of silk is not possible, place some small blocks of wood underneath the frame so that the silk is freely suspended. You can actually fix very large pieces of silk straight on to painting trestles, thus ensuring that the silk can have no contact with any surface beneath it. When restretching the silk, the trestles will have to be moved slightly.

FIXING

Brilliant and non-fading colours

Before it is fixed, silk painting is extremely delicate. A drop of water can ruin everything! Therefore you should fix the painting as soon as possible. Fixing means that the colours will not fade and they will be proof against washing and dry cleaning. Fixing also increases the intensity and brilliance of the colours, particularly when using steam. There are three fixing methods: steam fixing; electric iron fixing; and fixing using chemical solutions.

Experience shows that iron-fixable colours can also be fixed using the steam method. In such cases, however, spirit-based outliner must have been used. You must also fix using steam if you have painted a picture using a combination of iron-fixable colours and spirit-based outliner.

Electric iron fixing

Silk painted with iron-fixable colours must be allowed to dry thoroughly. Then fix the painting using an iron. Make sure you follow the manufacturer's instructions. Iron the painted silk on the reverse side for between four and five minutes. It is better to take too long when fixing than not long enough. Ironing also fixes coloured outliners at the same time. Follow the instructions for the colours and outliners as, before ironing, the paintings must be handled differently depending on the products used.

Steam fixing

The traditional, steam-fixable silk painting colours are fixed using steam, either in a pressure cooker or in a special fixing appliance. A fixing service for your silk paintings should be available locally.

Pressure cooker fixing

Fixing in a pressure cooker is risky because the silk can very easily come into contact with water. Place the silk painting on two layers of thick paper (do not use printed newspaper for this). Stroke the silk flat and then lay two further layers of paper on top of it; place the next piece of silk on top of that, followed by thick paper, and so on. Fold this into a packet or roll and form a helix. The height of the helix should not exceed 10 cm (4 in). Pour half a litre (1 pint) of water into the pressure cooker. The compartment should not be overfilled. Lay the packet on to the sieve and cover the top with aluminium foil so that the silk cannot come into contact with water. Seal the lid and steam under

pressure for approximately 45 minutes. Then allow the steam to escape and very carefully open the cooker. You can unpack the silk once it has cooled down. The painting is now fixed.

Fixing using a steamer

Fixing with a steamer is much simpler and entails far less risk. Various silk painting companies sell steamers. The picture shows the Hobby I, known in the UK as a 'horizontal steamer', for silk pieces up to 90 cm (36 in) wide and 18 m (20 yds) long. The Hobby II, or 'vertical steamer', can take silk pieces up to 140 cm (56 in) wide.

To fix using this method you need a steamer, two hot plates, absorbent paper on a roll, masking tape, aluminium foil and water. Stick the end of the paper roll on to the aluminium bar from the steamer. Wrap the paper two or three times around the bar. Make sure that the roll does not slip sideways. There should be approximately 5 cm (2 in) free at each end of the bar; this is the space needed to hang the bar in the steamer. Lay the silk painting flat and uncreased on to the paper **(1)**.

Lay a second roll of paper on to the silk painting. The two layers of paper absorb any excess colour. Now carefully roll the two paper layers, with the silk lying between them, on to the bar. No creases should appear in the silk. Make sure that you roll the silk straight. The maximum diameter of the roll must not exceed 10 cm (4 in). Roll a few additional layers of paper over the last painting to protect the silk from water droplets **(2)**.

Stick down the fixing roll length-

1

2

3

ways using masking tape and seal the ends well with aluminium foil. The foil should cover only the edges of the paper and not the silk. If steam cannot reach the silk, it will not be fixed. Pour 4 litres (8 pints) of water into the steamer. Then hang the roll in the steamer and close the lid. Turn the hot plate on to full heat until the first steam escapes. Then you can turn down the heat slightly; however, the water must continue to boil throughout. Depending on the thickness of the roll the fixing process will take between 60 and 90 minutes. After fixing, remove the fixing roll. Allow the roll to cool a little before unrolling the silk painting.

Dry clean the silk painting thoroughly in order to remove the spirit-based outliner **(3)**. We recommend that you use a specialist dry cleaning service for this.

Liquid fixing

Liquid-fixable colours are made light-fast and proof against washing and dry cleaning by applying a fixing solution after painting. After approximately two hours the liquid fixer can be rinsed out.

Washing out excess colour

After fixing, remove any excess colour and colourless outliner by washing out the silk in luke-warm water (approx. 30°C (86°F)) to which a dash of vinegar has been added. When washing the silk it must be continuously agitated so that no discoloration occurs. Wait several days before washing the silk again as even after fixing it can still take up colour.

To dry the silk, squeeze it a little and then hang it up in such a way that no two parts of the material are in contact.

THE STUDIO

Good light and a good mood

Painting is something for which you have a feel. To a large extent it is your mood that determines which colours you choose and whether or not you find the right flow for your brushstrokes. Therefore, make sure that you feel comfortable and at ease in your studio. It does not have to be a room given over solely to painting. All you need is a work surface on which you can leave your paintings and equipment, even when you are not actually painting. The main thing is that you have enough space for the frames and other tools that you need at the ready when painting.

The materials you need for painting with iron-fixable colours are shown below. For the traditional steam-fixable colours you will also need to have alcohol or thinner at the ready. The work surface and the floor should be washable so that the colour can be easily removed.

Things are so often dropped. If need be, a white oilcloth or a plastic sheet laid under the painting surface will do. When painting, old clothes are the order of the day; this means the odd splash will not matter so much.

Of course, light also has an important role to play. Where at all possible the source of light should come from the front, from above left (or from above right for left-handed painters) and it should illuminate the painting surface evenly. This will

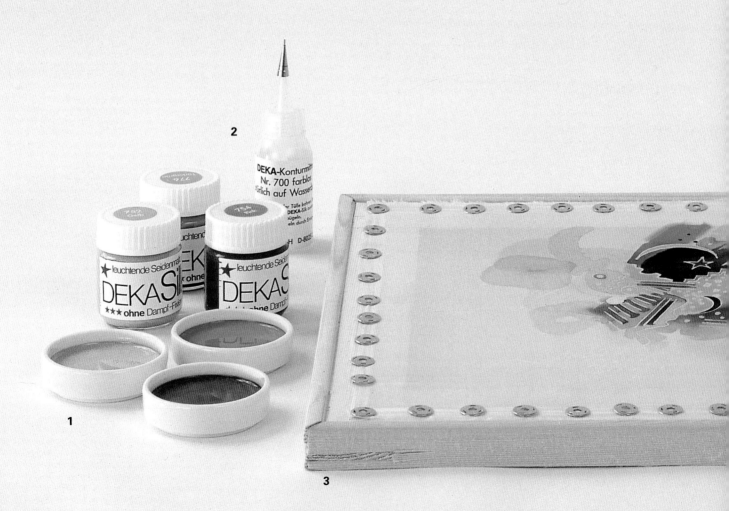

2

1

3

avoid any shadows which might otherwise hinder you when painting. The best position is near a window. Professional painters prefer a north-facing window because the light from the north is very neutral and hardly ever causes colour distortions. It is best to store the silk, colours and other paining tools in separate boxes.

Things you need at the ready when painting:

1 Colour bowls and colours already mixed. Make up larger amounts of colours in sealable jars such as jam jars.
2 Pipette bottle with outliner.
3 Frame with silk.
4 Two jars containing water: one for washing out brushes; one for diluting and rinsing and washing out colours. In areas of very hard water, use distilled water.
5 Porcelain or plastic colour palette for mixing colours. There is a wide range on the market. To begin with a white porcelain plate would suffice.
6 Brushes for colours and water.
7 Paper handkerchiefs for dabbing away water or excess colour and for cleaning brushes.
8 White paper or small photo frames with silk stretched across them for testing colour mixtures.
9 Glass drop counter with rubber sucker, used for colour mixing. For large amounts of colour use a plastic measuring beaker with a capacity up to 6 ml (1 tsp).

You should also have the following tools within easy reach:
– your sketch, so that you can compare it with your silk picture
– three-point pins for re-stretching the silk
– a hair dryer for watercolouring
– Essence F for thinning spirit-based outliner if the colours are to be fixed using steam
– salt for the salt technique

Painting on silk

Silk-painting is a fascinating art. Using brushes and colours you can create the most beautiful effects on silk, ranging from colours gently flowing into one another to clearly de-lineated designs, pastel watercolours or strong, brilliant colour tones. In this chapter you will be given an overview of the different silk painting techniques.

THE WORK STAGES

From design to silk painting

The stages for creating a silk painting follow a particular order. Below is a step-by-step guide to all the most important work stages, from the preliminary sketch to the finished picture.

Transferring the sketch on to the silk

Place the preliminary sketch on to tracing paper and stick it down using masking tape. Lay the silk over this, stretch it tightly using pins and trace the design using a soft pencil (3B) or preferably an 'Auto Fade Pen' **(1)**.

Drawing lines using outliners

Stretch the silk across your frame using three-point pins. Remember to seal the frame using masking tape before you stretch the silk across it so that the silk does not come into contact with previously used colours. The silk must be stretched tightly and must not sag. Then re-trace the lines on your silk using an outliner. Draw the lines evenly and as far as possible in one stroke to avoid gaps along the lines. The lines must be continuous because any gaps will let colour through during painting. Hold the silk up to the light. This will enable you clearly to identify any gaps in the outlines **(2)**.

Painting the silk

First, paint the maple leaf wet-on-wet (watercolour technique, see page 64). Paint the leaf design with water and then spread the following colours into one another: golden

yellow, olive green, claret red, turquoise and blue-green. Before applying, lighten the colours a little using water on a white porcelain plate and then test them on a piece of paper or silk. When painting, do not paint the colours too closely together; instead leave a little space between them and then spread the colours into one another using a watercolour brush. This makes the colour merging more attractive. When spreading colours into one another, do not allow them to dry as this will create distinct edges.

Next, paint the decorative design (for the colours to use see pictures 4, 5 and 6). Use a no 6 brush for the large areas and a no 3 brush for the detail.

Paint the stripes using a light turquoise. If necessary, and depending on the colour impression of the overall picture, you can later intensify the colour of the stripes using French blue.

Paint briskly using parallel strokes of the brush. Paint the intervening stripes wet-on-wet using golden yellow and claret red. Finally, add a few black strokes and then leave the whole thing to dry out thoroughly **(3)**.

Now all you need to do is fix, clean and iron your silk.

1

2

3

4

5

6

MATERIALS
Silk: 46 × 46 cm (18 × 18 in) crêpe de Chine
Colours: golden yellow, claret red, Madras red, turquoise, French blue, olive green, violet, blue-green, black
Brushes: sable brushes no 3 and no 6
Outliner: colourless spirit-based outliner
Techniques: outliner and watercolour

Maple leaf
Make a retracing of your preliminary sketch, using a colourless, spirit-based outliner (for the outliner technique see page 36) and then paint the areas wet-on-wet (see page 64). Make sure that the painting surface is always damp so that the colours can run into one another easily.

7

BASIC TECHNIQUES

Here you can see at a glance the effect of the various silk painting techniques. You can paint very clear forms or allow shapes and colours to merge into one another naturally – in silk painting, anything is possible.

Silk painting is based in the main on three basic techniques:
- outliner technique – see leaves 1, 2 and 3
- salt technique – see leaf 4
- watercolour technique – see leaves 5 and 6

All the techniques can easily be combined. This gives you an infinite number of creative design possibilities.

The individual techniques and the variations are explained in detail on the following pages. Each of the coloured areas of the leaves on this page has been painted using a different silk painting technique. The outer contours of the leaves, however, were all drawn using an outliner. The different silk painting techniques therefore relate only to the coloured areas.

Leaf 1 – white outlines
Outliners are liquids, with about the consistency of honey, which you can use for painting on silk. In those areas where you have used outliners the silk will not absorb any further colour. In other words, with an outliner you can clearly draw the entire outline of areas to be coloured. Outliners are either water-soluble (eg as supplied by Deka) or spirit-based (eg as supplied by Serti).

Using a colourless outliner, the leaf is drawn on to a piece of white silk and then painted with silk painting colours. This makes the outlines visible as they are the colour of the original silk, ie white. This technique can be used to create very attractive graphic effects.

Leaf 2 – coloured outlines
This leaf is drawn using a black outliner and then painted. The black outliner on a white background heightens the graphic effect. Outliners are available in many colours, such as gold, silver, green and pink.

1 white lines drawn with spirit-based outliner

2 black lines drawn with spirit-based outliner

3 colour-reserved lines drawn with spirit-based outliner

Leaf 3 – colour-reserved outliner lines

Here the silk is painted wet-on-wet with colour tones that merge into one another, before the outliner is applied. After the silk has dried completely, a colourless outliner is used to paint a random pattern over the colours. Use a spirit-based outliner for this technique.

Then a grey scumble or wash is applied over the leaf (see page 51 for instructions on how to do this). This makes those areas to which no outliner has been applied darker, and the outliner lines are retained in the original colours.

Leaf 4 – salt technique

This is a popular technique, particularly when painting flower designs; here chance plays an artistic role. With a little practice and experience you will have precise control over the salt technique effect.

It is very simple. Paint the silk and scatter salt on to it while it is still wet; allow the colours to dry and then remove the salt. The attractive shapes and patterns are created purely at random.

Leaf 5 – watercolour technique (Wet-on-wet painting)

Using this technique you can let the colours flow gently into one another. The important thing to note is that as they merge with one another the colours must be damp or wet; otherwise dark edges or water marks will occur. You can dampen the silk before you begin painting in order to facilitate the merging of the colours.

Firstly, mark the contours of the leaf with a colourless outliner, then paint the leaf wet-on-wet.

Leaf 6 – watercolour technique (washing out)

Using thinner or water, you can 'wash out' silk painting colours after the painting has dried. Draw the lines on to a piece of white silk using an outliner, and then paint the leaf. Once the painting has dried, wash out the colour using a thinner.

Using the basic techniques described above you will be able to create a great many designs often with surprising effects. Keep testing different ones. That is the best way to get to know the variety and potential of silk painting.

5 watercolour technique (wet-on-wet)

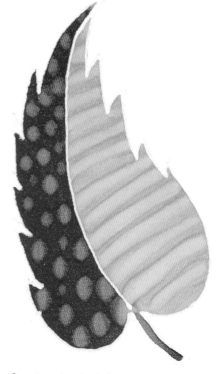

6 watercolour technique (washing out)

4 salt technique

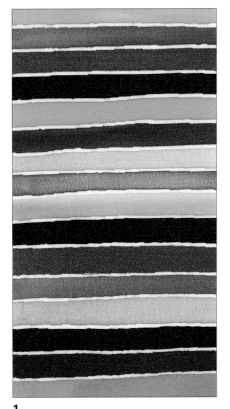

1

OUTLINER TECHNIQUES

Outliners

The diverse effects of silk painting are based in the main on two techniques: the watercolour technique with gently merging colours; and the outliner technique for clearly defined areas of colour.

The way in which outliners work is very simple. Areas to which you apply an outliner will not absorb any more colour. So, to begin with, you draw the outlines of the areas to be coloured using an outliner, let the whole thing dry, and then you paint the individual areas with silk painting colours.

A distinction is made between two different types of outliner, both of which have their own particular advantages and disadvantages. These are water-soluble outliners for iron-fixable colours, and spirit-based outliners for traditional, steam-fixable colours. The silk paintings shown in this book were done using both types of outliner.

Working with outliners

To draw, pour your outliners into a small pipette bottle fitted with a nib attachment. When you are not drawing, insert a thin wire into the nib attachment to stop the outliner from evaporating and the thin hollow needles from becoming blocked.

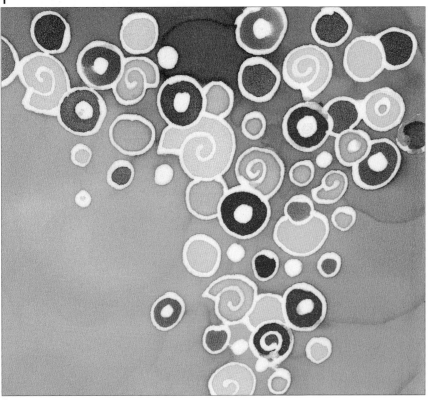

2

3

Straight lines

Draw a few straight, parallel lines on the silk using your pipette filled with outliner. The more quickly you work, the better the results will be. Draw the lines in a single stroke. If you stop and have to restart a line, this will cause a slight thickening.

Before you start to paint with colours, allow the outliners to dry thoroughly. After painting, fix and wash out or dry clean the painting **(1)**.

Circles and dots

Round shapes are somewhat more difficult to paint than straight lines because, as far as possible, you need to draw round an area, using an outliner, in one stroke while at the same time making sure that the circle is properly sealed. If the circle is not properly sealed, colour will invariably escape through the gap when you start to paint **(2)**.

Angular shapes

Here too it is important that all shapes are closed off and that no drops are allowed to form **(3)**.

Labyrinth

The separating lines cannot be seen on this picture. This attractive effect is easy to create. Paint a large area of your silk wet-on-wet in the desired colour tones – which should not be too dark – and allow the colour application to dry thoroughly. Then draw the shapes on to the colours using outliner and once they have dried, paint these areas black. Once fixing has been done and the outliner has been removed, the outlines can no longer be seen.

The recommended way to apply this hidden outliner is to work from light to dark **(4)**.

1 Straight lines – a simple basic exercise.

2 Circles and dots – here you must paint in continuous strokes.

3 Angular shapes – you need to ensure that all shapes are sealed.

4 Labyrinth – the outlines are not visible.

Painting with outliners

Lines are easy to draw if you fit a metal nib attachment to your pipette. The nib may typically have a diameter of 0.6 mm, as in the example shown. This allows you to paint very thin lines evenly. Position the pipette at an angle on the silk so that not too much and not too little outliner flows out. Before you begin work, force the air out of the neck of the pipette; this will prevent any bubbles forming **(1)**.

Drawing the lines
At first you may find that at the point where you placed the nib on to the silk, a drop has formed and the line here is thicker.

This can be avoided by using a piece of paper which you align with the starting point of the line you wish to draw on the silk. Place the pipette on the paper and then, in a single movement, draw the line from the paper on to the silk. Once the outliner lines have dried you can begin the main painting **(2 and 3)**.

Using a brush
Spirit-based outliner can also be applied using a brush (see picture 2 on page 8). To do this, the outliner needs to be thinned slightly. Depending on whether you want to mask wide areas or fine, detailed elements, such as grasses, choose a

2

3

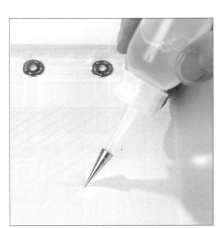

1

thick or a thin bristle brush. Paint in sweeping movements to make the forms more flowing (4).

Painting over with colours

The outliner must be thoroughly dry before you paint over it with colours. Now the forms become clearly visible (5 and 6). The outliner you choose will depend on how you want to paint; you should also use the correct dilutant for thinning.

A somewhat thicker outliner is well suited to drawing fine lines. A runny outliner is better for painting broader lines, areas and designs. Bristle brushes are the most suitable for this.

Practice using different consistencies of outliner before you begin in earnest. OIf the outliner is too thick it will not completely penetrate the silk and the lines can become unsealed. If the agent is too runny it may not adequately resist the colour.

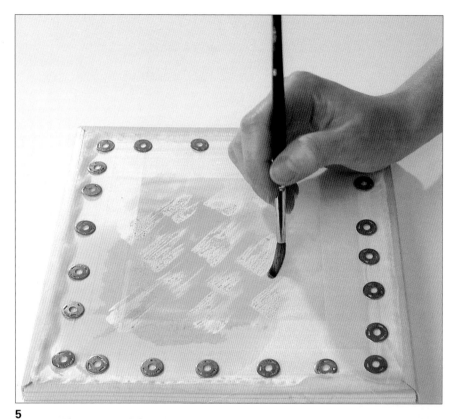

5

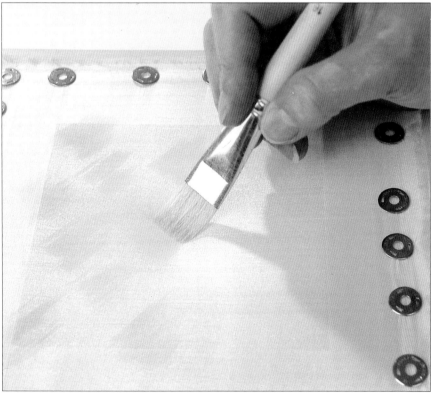

4

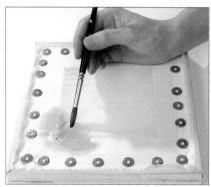

6

1 This is how to obtain the best lines: position the pipette at an angle and draw it evenly across the silk.

2 and **3** Paint the areas with colour.

4 You can also apply the outliner using a bristle brush.

5 and **6** As soon as colour is painted over it, wonderful designs become visible.

Painting with coloured outliners

You can paint radiant, iridescent accents with coloured outliners. The metallic, shining lines are particularly vivid on dark backgrounds. More colours have recently become available. Deka, for example, offer many different colour shades that are rendered wash-proof by electric-iron fixing. For these outliners, use the appropriate silk painting colours for iron fixing. In the case of gold and silver outliners, however, follow the manufacturer's guidelines precisely. Not all products are wash proof and dry cleaning proof.

You prepare coloured outliners in exactly the same way as colourless ones. Before you pour the outliner into the pipette, stir it thoroughly so that the colour particles are evenly distributed. Coloured outliners offer you an unusual effect in silk painting: you can paint over areas on which you have already worked. Therefore you can sometimes also use this type of outliner to cover up any errors you may have made. Make sure, however, that the coloured outliners always have a somewhat raised effect – in other words that they stand out clearly from the normal silk colours. If you have applied the coloured outliner too thickly the lines may stick to your ironing board when you come to iron the silk. If this happens, carefully pull the silk away from the ironing board. (You may wish to protect your ironing board with a piece of cloth to avoid marking it.) Immediately after painting, coloured outliners are sticky. They must be left to dry thoroughly on the silk.

MATERIALS
Outliners: gold, silver, black, green, blue, violet.

Jagged lines and circles
A playful abstract design, its charm lies in the contrast between round and jagged shapes; on a black background the shimmering colours have a particularly strong effect.

Paint a black background on to the silk and allow the colour to dry thoroughly. Then apply a lot of small, lively patterns to the silk using coloured outliners. So that you obtain a clear design, make sure that the shapes you paint are as compact as possible – in other words paint several parallel lines close to one an-

1

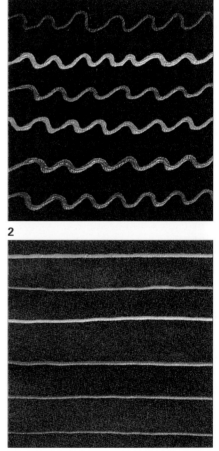

2

3

other, or small groups of recurring dots in the shape of a triangle, for example **(1)**.

Wavy lines on a black background

Dye the silk using black Deka-Silk and let the colour dry thoroughly. Then, using different coloured outliners, draw several wavy lines over the surface. Work swiftly and steadily. Before you fix the colours with an iron, allow the lines to dry thoroughly **(2)**. The wavy form will give the lines a shimmering effect, irrespective of the direction of light.

Lines on a black background

Instead of painting wavy lines, as in picture 2, paint parallel lines on to silk that has been dyed black **(3)**.

Black contours

Here, the first thing you must do is paint a pattern on to white silk using black outliner. Once this has dried, fill in the pattern with bright colours. By the use of this simple method you can create a strong, graphic effect **(4)**.

Silver waves and circles

Apply, wet-on-wet, a gently flowing blue-green background. Then wash out wavy lines using water and, using silver outliner, draw waves and circles on to the background. Fill in some of the circles with bright yellow and green shades. After each working stage, allow the silk to dry thoroughly **(5)**.

Black and colourless lines

You can create an attractive black and white graphic effect by combining colourless and black outliners. This gives the picture a light, playful feel. First apply the colourless outliner lines and then the silk painting colours. Finally, draw on the black lines **(6)**.

4

5

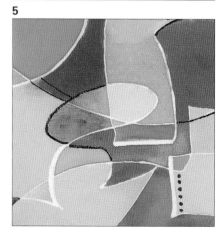

6

1 Coloured jagged shapes, lines and circles scattered across the black background like graffiti.

2 Paint wavy lines freely and boldly.

3 Straight lines create an attractive rainbow-like effect.

4 Black contours strengthen the colours' brilliance.

5 Shimmering silver lines brighten your picture.

6 Black and colourless lines create a playful, positive-negative effect.

1

Mistakes when painting with outliners

With any technique you are bound to make some mistakes! Even well-seasoned silk painting professionals have the occasional mishap. Here we show you how you can avoid mistakes and sometimes how to correct those you do make.

Outliners are a law unto themselves. Frequently they are too viscous or too runny; they drip and smudge, or they form air bubbles during painting. Consequently the outliners are not sealed, thus allowing colour to flow from one area to another.

Outliner lines drawn too quickly and too thinly. The colour runs **(1)**.
Remedy: Do not draw the lines too hastily; draw them steadily and evenly, allowing the outliner fully to penetrate the silk. Make sure that the outliner is not too viscous. If necessary, thin it slightly. Shake the outliner and the thinner well and then allow it to stand for a while; spirit-based outliner will need to stand for about half an hour, water-soluble outliner for about five minutes. This will allow any air bubbles that have formed in the pipette to escape.

There are air bubbles in the outliner **(2)**. Here, too, colour will run because the air bubbles mean that the outline is not completely closed.
Remedy: Before you begin to paint, squeeze the air bubbles out of the pipette on to a paper handkerchief and wipe the nib thoroughly.

Outliner has been smudged with the hand, starting points are not sealed and there are air bubbles **(3)**.
Remedy: You can discover this mistake before you begin painting with colour by holding up the silk to the light. This will enable you to see the outlines more clearly. When drawing lines make sure that, where at all possible, you work from the top left to the bottom right. This will lessen the risk of your hand smudging lines that are still wet.

Coloured outliner runs. The outliner is too runny **(4)**.
Remedy: This mistake can be avoided by stirring the outliner thoroughly.

Black outliner does not properly penetrate the silk and is lumpy **(5)**.
Remedy: The outliner is too viscous and needs to be thinned slightly and then well stirred.

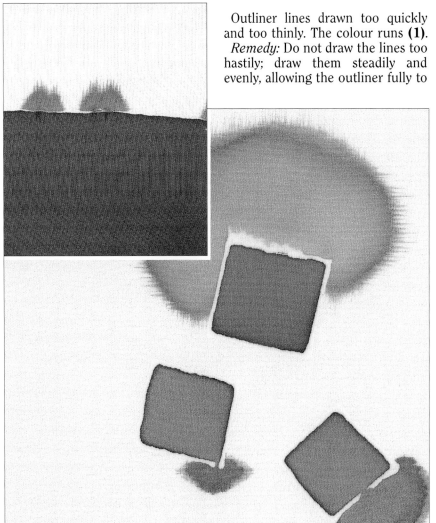

2 and 3

Correcting mistakes

You can rectify colour runs by dabbing them with a cotton-wool bud soaked in thinner; then leave the run to dry and paint the background darker so that the overrun disappears into it. However, this does not work with water-soluble outliners because the dabbing can cause them to dissolve and thus render them permeable. You can correct bad outlines with coloured outliners where this fits in artistically with your painting and where you have used a water-soluble, colourless outliner. However, you must first fix the picture and then remove the old outliner by washing. This will make all the colours slightly lighter. In picture 3, for example, you could paint over the offending lines with pink, gold and silver coloured outliner and then paint the background out-

5

side the square black in order to cover up the accidental colour run. If you are unable to remove a mistake, consider whether and how the mistake can be incorporated into your design.

Tip: Build up a file containing examples of your mistakes, recording how the error occurred and which outliner and colour you were using.

4

SUMMER MEADOW

Ribwort and dandelion sway in the wind – a meadow, with its gentle green grasses and small pink flowers that only grow in the wild, arousing many childhood memories. This is an ideal design for silk painting, which can enable you, unlike almost any other technique, to capture the mood of a meadow in the sunlight. The diverse and delicate plant forms are perfect candidates for the use of the outliner technique. Using silk painting colours you can achieve the most subtle colour nuances and shades. On the following pages you will see, step by step, precisely how such silk paintings are created.

Look very carefully at the pictures and read these pages thoroughly; then nothing should go wrong. It is advisable to test the various colours on a small piece of silk first.

Colour sketch

Begin with a colour sketch (below). Capture the movement of the grasses bending in the wind, and the glow of the colours in the sunlight. All you need for the draft is a coloured pencil sketch in which you develop the shapes and colours. Keep altering the sketch until it captures just the right mood. The colour sketch is important because there is a limit to the amount of adjustment you can make to the shapes and colours you later apply to the silk itself.

Transfer sketch

Using a pencil, transfer from your colour draft the outlines of the flowers and plants (see above). These are the lines that you will later paint on the silk using outliner. Any shapes should be sealed off so that no colour can run out of them. You can use this transfer sketch to enlarge the design as you transfer it on to the silk (see page 115). Many designs in this book are reproduced on a scale of 1:1; so too is the finished meadow picture (see page 49). You can therefore transfer all the lines on to the silk directly from this picture **(2)**.

Remember that you will need to leave a 3–5 cm (1¼–2 in) edge around the design when you draw it on the silk; this is to allow you to fix the silk to the frame. The design it-

1

self must always lie within the frame. The technique for transferring the design on to the silk has already been explained (see full instructions on page 32).

Next, stretch the silk across the frame as tightly as possible, making sure that it does not sag in the middle. (For the best results, stretch it as tight as a drum.)

Drawing the design using outliner

Using the outliner, draw the blades of grass from the bottom upwards, in the same direction as they grow. This is the best way to render the natural movement of the plants and to achieve a line that becomes ever finer as it progresses.

Make sure that each starting point is well sealed so that later no colour can flow out at these points **(1)**. Hold the silk up to the light if you are not sure; this should make it easier to see.

Painting pink flowers

Once the outliner has dried out thoroughly you can paint the small flowers using pink. Use a fine no 3

sable brush. It must have a very delicate tip. You must ensure that you do not take up too much colour with the brush; it is advisable just to dip the tip of the brush into the colour. The metal shaft should not come into contact with thinner, water or colour. This could cause liquid unexpectedly to run on to the painting and ruin it. Work very carefully so that you paint only within the confines of the outlines **(2)**.

Dandelions

The dandelion is somewhat larger. Here you can work with a no 6 brush. First, paint the flower yellow. Then shade the individual petals with a mixture of yellow and claret red, thus giving depth to the flower **(3)**.

MATERIALS

Colours: pink, yellow, lavender, claret, pistachio, green, olive green, turquoise, blue
Outliner: colourless
Brushes: Sable brushes nos 3 and 6
Technique: outliner technique

2

Bottom left: Set out on the colour sketch the colour distribution. This will enable you to assess the eventual effect of the silk painting.

Top left: The transfer sketch shows you all the outliner lines that you will have to transfer to the silk.

1 The lines are drawn on using outliner.

2 Carefully paint the pink flowers using the tip of the brush.

3 You can paint the dandelion using a thicker brush.

3

Painting the ribwort

The delicate panicles (ears) of the ribwort are painted using pink and yellow. Here you must work very carefully. The shape of the panicles is made up of small strokes of outliner which are open at the sides, representing the tiny, gentle hairs. Colour can easily run through these gaps. Therefore use a delicate no 3 sable brush and keep the work as dry as possible by taking up only a small amount of colour on to the brush each time. Before you paint, make the first stroke of the brush on absorbent paper. Only then should you paint the colour into the panicle. Then paint the small points of colour between the yellow blades.

Shading the pink flowers

Here, too, you will need to work with a very dry and delicate brush. At the edge of the larger of the small pink flowers, right up against the outline, paint a slightly darker coloured line in claret. Then work from the centre of the flower using a little water so that the claret red is forced up against the outliner edge, thus creating a gentle colour transition from the middle of the flower to the edge **(4)**.

Covering the panicles

Paint over the pink of the panicles with outliners so that later, when the background is applied, no colour runs into them **(5)**.

Painting the leaves and grasses green

Paint using a no 3 or no 6 brush, depending on the size of the leaf. Mix the green tones using blue and yellow, and lighten individual tones using water, thus creating a whole palette of delicately graded green shades. The more shades, the better. Later, the effect of this will be to enliven the leaf. Then paint all the leaves and grasses. In so doing you can let all the colour tones run into one another, wet-on-wet **(6)**.

Painting the background

Painting this background is not particularly easy. If you have little experience of silk painting it is advisable to paint the entire background in one colour, blue for example. Before you start to paint the background, carefully cover the very delicate grasses, smaller flowers and yellow dots with outliner. If you have used a spirit-based outliner for the picture, when painting the background you can paint freely over the covered parts because spirit-based outliner does not dissolve. This is not the case, however, if you have used a water-soluble outliner. Here you have to be somewhat more careful when applying the colour. Paint the background as accurately as possible around the outlines so that they are not dissolved by the wet colour.

Paint the background blue from the bottom to the top up to the natural outliner border created by the plant shapes growing over one another **(7)**.

4

5

4 The dark edges give the flower a three-dimensional appearance.

5 Use a delicate metal nib for covering the panicles with outliner.

6 Gentle green-yellow breathes life into the leaves.

7 The background of the summer meadow is drawn from the bottom to the top and gets lighter the higher up the picture you go.

6 and 7

Painting the background wet-on-wet

The picture is almost finished. Only the upper part of the background is still to be done. So that you can quickly paint the background with the colours flowing into one another, take blue, turquoise, lavender, yellow and pink and, using a dropper, place a few drops of each into troughs in a paint-mixing palette. Then quickly paint the upper part of the picture with water. Brush the water into the grasses and as far as the outliner lines.

Do not use too much water! Before you begin painting with colours, allow the water to dry slightly so that the colours do not flow into one another too much.

The silk must still be damp, however. Now brush the various colours in to the area. If necessary dilute the colours a little in advance. Keep the colour areas slightly damp at the edge using a second water-

colour brush so that they do not dry out and form edge marks. Start with yellow and paint a very light pink tone at the side of this. This creates a warmer yellow against the blue.

Make sure, as far as possible, that the blue and yellow do not flow together in the background, thus avoiding any resulting green **(8)**.

You obtain a particularly striking effect if the soft blue and yellow parts of the background run diagonally to the perpendicular axis of the plants. Make sure that, as far as possible, you apply the brushstrokes in an arc from the bottom left to the top right. This emphasises the stretching movement of the grasses and flowers towards the light.

You must now fix the painting, according to the type of outliner you have used, and then remove the outliner. In the case of water-soluble outliners, use an electric iron for fixing and then wash out the silk painting. If you have used spirit-based outliner you will have to fix using

steam and then have the painting cleaned by a dry-cleaning specialist.

Only now will you be able to appreciate the full effect of the picture. There is no longer any outliner covering the colours. Depending on the colour tones, you will now see either an intense, glowing brilliance or subtle, gentle pastels on the softly shimmering silk.

If, to begin with, you are not confident enough to reproduce the entire design, transfer just a few grasses and plants and paint these as a test sample.

This should provide you with sufficient practice, and you will soon be ready to paint your summer meadow on to silk.

In this picture, colours, shapes and forms create a very attractive overall impression. This is because, in spite of the many small shapes and areas, the picture is built up very simply. In the main the colours run along a gentle arc, from the bottom left to the top right. This lends the design a natural dynamism which further emphasises the vitality of the leaves, grasses and flowers.

8 The background, painted wet-on-wet with colours flowing into one another, requires some practice. You could also paint the background in just one colour, for example a gentle blue.

9 The silk painting has been fixed and cleaned. The summer meadow is complete. The flowers and grasses sway gently in the sunlight. Through the movement of the lines from bottom left to top right the picture exudes a mood of bright optimism which is further emphasised by the carefully harmonized colours.

OVERLAYING TECHNIQUE

Attractive effects painted layer by layer

You can create quite amazing effects using the overlaying technique. You will need some practice with colours and outliners before attempting larger designs. Begin by doing a few test samples; after that it should not be difficult for you to achieve good results. The principle of the overlaying technique is very simple: you paint an area with colour and then mask part of that area using spirit-based outliner. Then you apply another layer of colour over that. In those areas that you have masked, nothing will happen; the first colour will be retained. But in areas to which you have not applied spirit-based outliner, the new colour layer will alter the original colour. To use this technique you will need some experience and knowledge of how colours change as a result of overpainting.

A few basic rules

Always start with the palest colour and make each subsequent layer darker than the previous one. In silk painting, overpainting can only make colours darker, not lighter. You can test how this happens using a small piece of silk.

The more colours from one colour-tone series you paint over one another, the subtler the colour nuances achieved.

Only spirit-based outliner, used in conjunction with the appropriate steam-fixable colours, is suitable for the overlaying technique.

Colours and outliner must be thoroughly dry before you begin the next stage of work. If they are not, damp outliner may be partly dissolved by the new layer of colour, leading to the colour penetrating the silk at that point and changing it quite dramatically.

If you want to mask large areas, use a broad bristle brush to apply the outliner. You can thin the outliner with a little Essence F. The design on this page is a good practice exercise for beginners.

Creating a picture layer by layer

Use a small format for this picture, 30 × 30 cm (12 × 12 in) for example.

Before you begin painting, dilute the colours in small bowls using a lot of water and make up the various shades. Lemon becomes warmer if you mix a little ruby red with it. All the colours used in this exercise are mixtures. You can read about mixing colours in the chapter entitled 'The

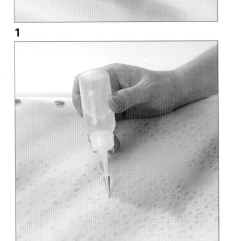

1

2

3

4

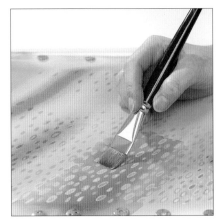

5

World of Colours' (beginning on page 84).

For the first layer of colour apply the palest possible shades with a lot of water. For the next layer, deepen the colours by adding a little more of the basic colour to the colour mixture.

You deepen pale yellow, for example, by adding pure yellow. Before you start a new layer, the previous one must have dried thoroughly.

Paint an area, wet-on-wet, using pale colour shades diagonally across the silk (**1**).

Use spirit-based outliner to create oval dots and circles (**2**).

Using a flat brush, paint on a second, slightly darker colour run. Make sure that you keep to the order of colours already set. In other words, apply the same colours over each other, ie turquoise over turquoise, lemon over lemon, etc (**3**).

Use spirit-based outliner to mask old and create new circles and dots (**4**).

Apply a third, still darker, layer of colour (**5**).

Now, for the third time, use spirit-based outliner to mask a few circles and dots (**6**).

Finally, paint a grey scumble or wash over the picture. To do this, dilute black silk painting colour using water until an attractive medium-grey shade is created. You can darken the grey using black if you find that the contrast is not strong enough. The masked colour shades are now set off attractively (**7**).

After painting, allow the picture to dry thoroughly, fix it and clean it.

Variation: Apply the spirit-based outliner using a bristle brush. This creates attractive patterns.

MATERIALS
Silk: 30 × 30 cm (12 × 12 in) habutai silk or crêpe de Chine
Colours: steam-fixable colours – turquoise, ruby red, lemon, sky blue, black
Brushes: sable brush no 7 or no 9
Outliner: spirit-based outliner
Technique: overlaying technique

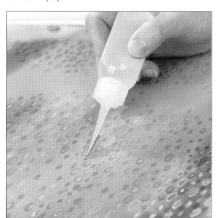

6

7

SKYLINE

MATERIALS
Silk: 60 × 60 cm (24 × 24 in) crêpe de Chine
Colours:
Colour chart, top row: blue, orange, silver grey, black
Colour chart, middle row: turquoise blue, turquoise green, crimson, lavender
Colour chart, bottom row: yellow, pink, claret red, violet
Brushes: sable brushes nos 3 and 8
Outliner: spirit-based outliner
Technique: overlaying technique

The big city is enticing. It effervesces with life, colour and excitement. The sky glows brightly, reflecting the city lights. The silhouettes of the skyscrapers – the skyline – dominates the scene. This picture draws its life from a few creative characteristics. The graphic effect of the vertical lines of the upward-reaching skyscrapers is reinforced by the lightly applied diagonal background. The atmospheric background thus contrasts with the clearly defined high-rises, and it is this creative tension that is the very essence of the picture.

You can see this colourful picture on page 57. On the pages that pre-cede it we show you, step-by-step, how to paint the design using the overlaying technique.

Begin with the initial drawing. How to transfer and enlarge the draft depicted in the bottom left-hand corner of this page has already been explained (see also page 115).

All the colours used in this picture are shown at the bottom right-hand corner of this page.

First, apply the background. To begin with paint the coloured stripes, wet-on-wet, in parallel, diagonal brushstrokes on to the silk. Use the colours turquoise blue, pink and yellow which you dilute in a small bowl using water. Have sufficient diluted colour at the ready so that it does not run out while you are painting. It is almost impossible to remix the exact colour tone a second time.

Leave a small white gap between each stripe of colour.

The colours must dry thoroughly before you begin to apply the spirit-based outliner (**1**).

Now draw the draft on to the silk using spirit-based outliner. The design has a clearly defined structure. It is made up predominantly of vertical and horizontal lines. The lines should run as parallel as possible. You can make the job simpler by first painting all the vertical lines,

then all the horizontal lines, then the roofs, then the windows, then the ornamentation and house façades. Draw the lines as steadily as possible, applying the same amount of pressure and without removing the brush during the painting of each line.

Be careful not to smudge any outliner lines that are still damp as you paint (**2**).

Once the outliner has dried thoroughly, use a delicate no 3 brush to paint in the windows. You will see which colours to apply where by looking at the picture on page 57. As the areas involved are very small,

do not take up too much colour into the brush. Use the tip of the brush carefully to paint in the windows. You can use the colours as they are. In this instance you do not need to dilute or mix them (**3**).

1 Paint the background quickly, wet-on-wet.

2 All shapes must be edged using outliner and there must be no gaps in the lines, otherwise during painting the colour will run out of the shapes.

3 You create the big city lights using many bright colours.

1

2

3

Use yellow and orange and a little crimson to paint the decoration on the cupola.

These colours too can be used in their original shades. If you do not have orange, make up the colour by mixing together yellow and red. Orange lends the picture warmth.

Next paint all the house façades, excluding the black areas (**4**).

Use spirit-based outliner to apply a few dots to the background and let them dry thoroughly. These dots will later appear in the pale colour shades.

Now apply the second colour layer to the background. To do this, add a little turquoise blue, pink and yellow to the appropriate colour bowls in order to intensify or deepen the colours. If you have already used up all your diluted colour for the background, remix the colour, this time using a little less water.

In the main you should create the background using the same method as that described on pages 50 and 51. There is, however, one difference: because you cannot paint the background as a whole and have to work around the silhouettes of the skyscrapers, you should use water to dampen the background thoroughly before you begin painting. Apply the water with a brush as if you were actually painting the background. This is important as it stops the colours drying out during painting and thus forming edge marks. This could easily happen as it will take you a little time to paint around the detailed silhouette shapes. Paint several colours, wet-on-wet, into one another. As water is first applied to the background you can in fact mix your colour shades slightly darker. The water will lighten the colours slightly. The best thing to do is test this effect on a small piece of silk (**5**).

Once the colours have dried, mask some more dots on the background. Leave plenty of room between the

4

5

dots, however, so that you can add some more later (**6**).

As soon as the outliner has dried thoroughly you can paint another colour layer over the background.

As with picture 5, mix the colours a shade darker. Once again, dampen the silk well and draw the lines diagonally in the appropriate colours across the background.

You can repeat this process several times. The more layers you paint, the more lively the effect will be. You do not have to follow these instructions slavishly; they are intended merely as a source of ideas and inspiration.

Experiment and try out your own ideas. Only then will you develop your own techniques. Often mistakes and unsuccessful experiments will reveal new ideas that you can then specifically apply later. This is particularly true of the overlaying technique, the full effects of which become apparent only after much practice. Particularly if you are mixing colours actually on the silk because you are overpainting – as with the overlaying technique – you should expect a few surprises.

The colour effect is dependent on many conditions, such as the type of silk being used, the manufacturer of the colours, and the dampness of the background and colours (**7**).

6

7

The picture is almost finished. All you have to do now is paint in the black contours of the buildings. This may look easy but it is not. You have to work very carefully to avoid the black running over the fine outliner lines. It is normally at this stage, just when you think the picture is almost complete, that most of the errors occur. Therefore, play it safe. Only take up a little colour into the brush and paint the small areas very carefully using the tip of the brush (**8**).

You can now roughly see the overall effect of the picture. It becomes even more radiant once it has been

8

9

fixed and cleaned, not least because the spirit-based outliner, which dulls the intensity of the colours, is removed. The final stage is to darken the background using a grey colour.

To do this, mix two or three shades of grey. As in the previous steps, paint the background with water and then, in parallel diagonal lines, apply the various grey tones to the damp area. This really brings to life the buildings and the dots in the sky (**9**).

Now you have the final picture; its brilliance is intensified as a result of fixing and cleaning (**10**).

You could, of course, use the same design with different colours. You might use grey, green, blue and white with a few reddish-yellow shades in the windows. This creates a mysterious wintry atmosphere in which the warm reddish-yellow tones are further emphasised by the cold greys, greens and blues.

This design is particularly suitable for experimenting with colours because its graphic make-up provides an effective structure from the very outset. Make sure that the foreground, from the point of view of the colours used, clearly contrasts with the background, as this picture draws its life not least from the carefully coordinated colour contrasts which can be achieved particularly well using the overlaying technique. You could also paint the design using a black outliner on a single-colour background.

SALT TECHNIQUE

Painting with salt

Bizarre shapes, fantastic flowers and exotic landscapes appear on the silk as if by magic; and salt makes it all possible. It is very simple. You place a few grains of salt on colours that are still wet on your silk painting and immediately delicate patterns begin to form. The salt grains absorb the moisture and the colours dissolve in it. The effect is that the salt lightens the colours surrounding it. Sometimes, however, the colours flow into strong rays, circles and other shapes reminiscent of flowers. Some of the colour pigment collects at the point of the actual salt grains, which leads to points of strong coloration.

You can control the effect by placing each individual grain of salt on to the silk using a pair of tweezers. Usually the colour flows towards the salt. A single grain will often create flame-like or flower-like shapes.

Ray-like streaks are formed if several grains are placed closely together. The shapes created depend on the degree of dampness and the composition of the colours, and on how you arrange the salt grains. Even the direction of the weave of the material can affect the flow of the colour. Often the direction of the absorption effect of the salt corresponds to the tension of the silk, ie the ray-shaped streaks appear to reach outwards towards the frame.

You can use ordinary table salt, coarse sea salt or specially-prepared salt – 'effect salt' – available from silk painting suppliers. Effect salt grains are larger and make stronger patterns than table salt.

Experiment as much as possible so that you are not taken unawares by any results you may get. Salt can, for example, break down some colour mixtures into their individual colour components. It can turn some shades of brown into red and green. This is all to do with the different flow speeds of the colours. The absorption capacity of the salt does have its limits, however. The greater the amount of colour, the less the salt effect. And damp salt has almost no effect.

The following technique has proved very successful for painting with salt. As you paint with your right hand and, using the left hand, immediately place the individual grains of salt on to the damp area of colour. As the grains' absorption capacity lasts for a while, you cannot move the grains on the damp silk. If you do, they will leave lines. Once the colour has dried, brush away the salt with a soft brush or a thick paintbrush so that it does not eat into the silk.

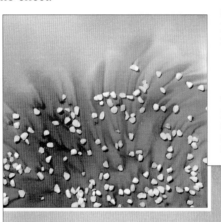

You can see clearly where the salt grains have been placed as they create darker spots of colour. Attractive, fountain-shaped patterns are formed using this method.

1 and 2

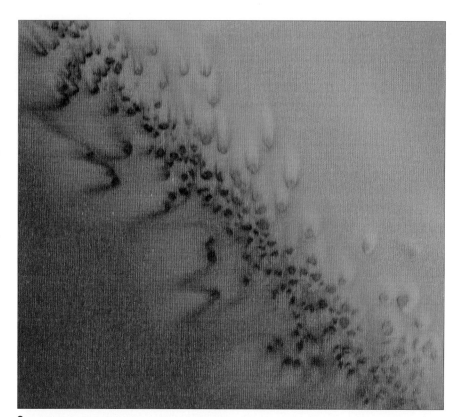

Materials
Silk: 18 × 16 cm (7 × 6½ in) crêpe
de Chine
Colours: steam-fixable silk painting
colours
Salt: Deka effect salt
Technique: salt technique

Paint a stroke, wet-on-wet, using diluted colour. As soon as the colour
has dried a little but is still damp,
draw stronger colour shades from
the lower part of the picture into
the top part using fountain-shaped
brush movements. Once in the upper part of the picture, the colours
should merge gently. Spread salt
grains on to the damp colour in line
with the flow; place more grains
below and fewer grains above (**1**).

Once the colour has dried thoroughly, brush away the salt. Attractive, fountain-shaped patterns will
have formed (**2**).

Draw a diagonal stroke using claret
red and blue-green. Scatter a thick
row of salt grains on to the damp
colour along the diagonal; the
grains should be less dense at the
upper and lower ends of the diagonal. Allow the picture to dry and
then brush away the salt (**3**).

In this picture you can clearly see
how the used salt has thoroughly
absorbed the colours (**4**).

3

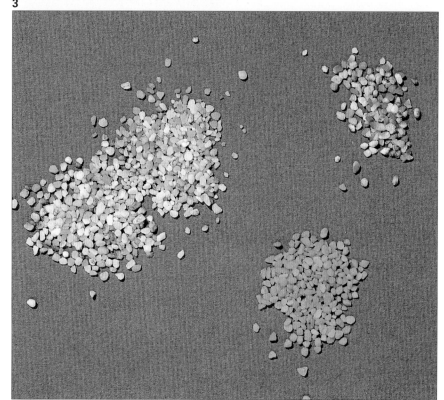

4

On these pages you will see how you can use salt deliberately to achieve specific effects.

MATERIALS
Silk: 20 × 20 cm (8 × 8 in) crêpe de Chine
Colours: steam-fixable silk painting colours red and yellow
Salt: Deka effect salt
Brush: no 8 sable brush
Technique: salt technique

Wet-on-wet, draw several parallel lines using red and yellow. Where the two colours meet, orange will be formed. Along each of the wet colour runs lay a straight row of individual salt grains (**1**).

Allow the colours to dry thoroughly and then brush away the salt. The salt will have created very attractive shapes, each of which will be pointing towards the edge of the silk. An attractive graphic effect is created by the parallel lines of comet-shaped forms which contrast well with the horizontal lines of colour (**2**).

MATERIALS
Silk: 20 × 20 cm (8 × 8 in) habutai
Colours: Steam-fixable silk painting colours red, yellow and blue
Salt: Deka effect salt
Brush: no 8 sable brush
Technique: salt technique

Paint a large yellow dot in the middle of the silk. Then paint a light red circle, wet-on-wet, around this dot and drop a light-red dot into the middle of the yellow dot. Scatter two circles of effect salt on to the colour. Then paint the remaining area of the silk blue and use the brush to push some of the blue colour towards the outer ring of salt. Allow the picture to dry thoroughly before removing the salt. The salt will create a flower-like effect (**3**).

MATERIALS
Silk: 20 × 20 cm (8 × 8 in) crêpe de Chine
Colours: steam-fixable silk painting colours red, yellow and blue
Salt: Deka effect salt
Brush: no 8 sable brush
Technique: salt technique
Wet-on-wet, draw several runs of colour and scatter several pinches of salt grains on to the wet colour. This results in many shapes, each one having an effect on the next and all of which point outwards towards the edge of the picture (**4**).

Colours do not mix with salt
Make sure that salt never comes into contact with colours that you have not yet applied to silk and which you still wish to use. Just one grain of salt can render your colours unusable. Even the brush you have been using for salt work can spoil your colours. Therefore, always wash out your brushes thoroughly before dipping them into your bottles of colour. Those colours that you intend to use with salt should be poured into a separate jar before you begin working. In this way you can protect the remaining colour from salt.

Another effect that you should be aware of is the following: when painting, colour runs around areas that have been treated with salt. Therefore, as it is very difficult to paint over areas on which salt has been scattered, do not use the salt until the final painting stage.

Silk painting is fascinating, not least because you can combine all the various techniques in one painting. The salt technique can therefore be used in conjunction with the outliner and watercolour techniques (**5**).

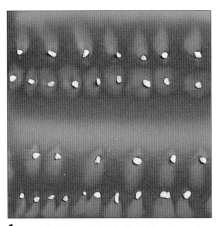

1

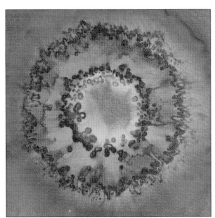

3

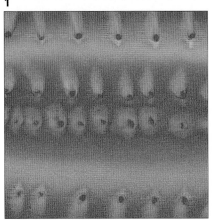

2

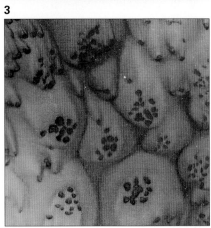

4

own creativity. Salt can only strengthen an idea; it cannot replace it. You can use salt for accentuation, but the idea for the picture should come from you.

On the other hand, the salt technique offers you much scope for experimentation. The random nature of the method is very stimulating. Play with the technique. Experiment as much as you like and then use the salt to create deliberate effects.

MATERIALS
Silk: 50 × 50 cm (20 × 20 in) habutai silk
Colours: steam fixable silk painting colours
Salt: Deka effect salt (only in picture 5)
Brushes: sable brushes nos 9 and 3
Techniques: salt technique and outliner technique

5

6

You should be aware that the effect created by using salt is very strong and bold; in other words, use salt sparingly. In picture 5 salt has only been used to create the background. It gives the design an irregular, random quality. The colours appear to be shooting out of the flowers – in total contrast to the tranquillity of the same design in picture 6. Therefore, use salt only for the primary feature of the design or only for the background (picture 5). Using salt is a very good method of delineating areas. With a little experience you will be able to assess the effect in advance. In the main, the shapes pull away from one another and towards the edge of the picture.

Unfortunately, a common mistake is to expect the effects created by the use of salt to substitute for one's

ZIGZAG

The picture shows how you can use simple tools which express strength and great tension.

A jagged line and the three primary colours – red, yellow and blue – plus the mixed colour turquoise are the creative elements that make up this design. All the colour surfaces have their own character. Yellow has a calming effect; the jagged red line exudes dynamism; and the salt effects on the blue area are invigorating.

MATERIALS
Silk: 40 × 60 cm (16 × 24 in) habutai silk
Colours: steam-fixable silk painting colours
Top row of colour chart: ruby red, lemon
Bottom row of colour chart: turquoise, sky blue
Brushes: sable brushes nos 3 and 8
Outliner: spirit-based outliner
Salt: Deka effect salt
Techniques: salt technique and outliner technique

Transfer the zigzag line on to the silk (**1**).

Go over the lines with spirit-based outliner. Be sure to close up all the lines; if this is not done properly your colours will flow into one another. There is a particular danger of small gaps in the corners. Draw the lines quickly but evenly so that the lines do not become too thin. Once the outliner has dried, paint in the stripe using red (**2**).

Mix a little ruby red into the lemon, thus making a warmer shade. Then paint the orange area.

Next add a little turquoise colour to the sky blue and paint, wet-on-wet, the other area.

Then, as quickly as possible, scatter grains of salt on to the blue area while the colour is still damp. You will now witness a wonderful change: light patches will form because the salt absorbs the colour, so the colour pigment is drawn towards the grains of salt. At the same time the blue to which you added turquoise, separates out again into blue and turquoise. This is because the blue and turquoise pigment move at different speeds towards the salt grains. The pigment is then deposited at the salt grains, at which point the silk darkens. Allow the colours to dry thoroughly and then brush away the grains of salt (**3**).

Now all that is left to do is to steam fix the silk painting and clean it. Cleaning and fixing will further enhance the salt effect (**4**).

1

2

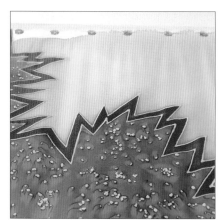

3

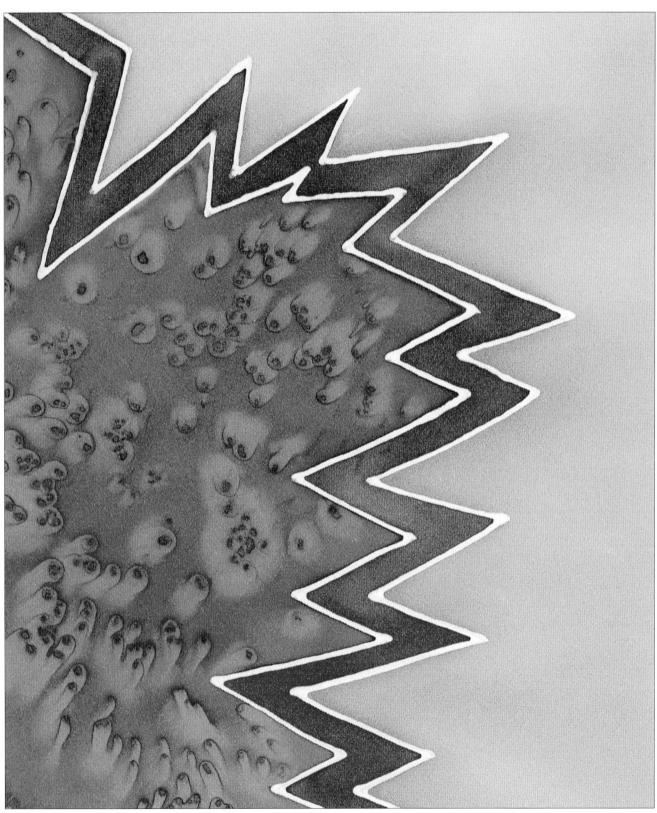

WATERCOLOUR TECHNIQUE

Flowing colour painted wet-on-wet

The watercolour technique is perhaps the most varied of the silk painting methods. If you love free-form shapes and like working with a paintbrush, the watercolour technique is for you. Without the restrictions of outliners the colours flow on the damp silk creating wonderful patterns and mixtures. You can, however, also create distinct contours by painting wet colours on to dry colours. The course of colours, water and thinner can be controlled easily using a hair dryer.

The watercolour technique offers several creative possibilities: there is the wet-on-wet technique; the thinner or wash-out technique; and the painting on primers technique.

You can, of course, combine all the techniques. In this way you will obtain a whole range of painting effects. You can see a few examples on these two pages. On the following pages you will find basic exercises in each of the techniques. You should practise these before attempting to paint the examples on these two pages.

Keep experimenting. Log your experiments, recording how you painted each one. In this way you will soon build up a repertoire of different ways to express yourself in your painting.

Painting wet-on-wet

As its name suggests, wet-on-wet painting means you paint on wet silk using fairly runny colour.

In addition, before painting you should wet the silk by applying water using a broad brush or a sponge. Do not allow pools of water to form, however. If they do, they should be mopped up immediately with kitchen paper.

During painting, the silk must not dry out as this could lead to the formation of edge marks. You must therefore work quickly and, if necessary, re-dampen the silk during the actual painting process.

Everything flows
(wet-on-wet painting)
Dampen the silk thoroughly using water. Paint from one side of the picture towards the middle using blue, and from the other side towards the middle using yellow. In the centre, pull the two colours together; the mixing of the colours will create a green area (**1**).

Colour tones
(wet-on-wet painting and the outliner technique)
First, draw the outliner lines and allow them to dry. Then dampen the silk thoroughly with water and paint on a few colour runs using several

1

2

colours. In this picture the colour run extends inside the area which is formed by the actual outliner lines. The design shows how attractive it can be when various techniques are combined (**2**).

Intoxication
(wash-out technique and wet-on-wet painting)
Brush water over the silk and paint, wet-on-wet, a blue-green flow. Allow the entire picture to dry thoroughly. Using a brush and water or thinner, wash out some small and large dots. The edges will form automatically, because the colour is driven out by the thinner. At the point at which the colour dries, dark lines will form (**3**).

Tracks
(wash-out technique and wet-on-wet painting)
Paint a yellow-red flow wet-on-wet. Allow it to dry thoroughly. Once it is

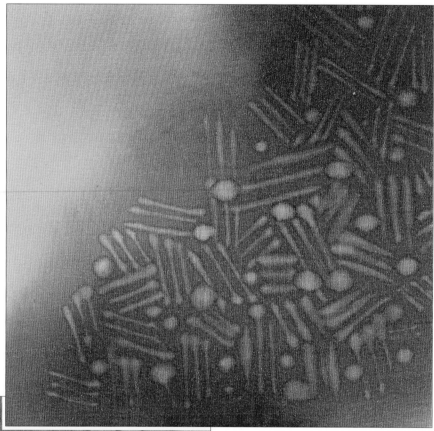

4

dry use a brush and water or thinner to wash out dots and stripes. This creates fascinating patterns (**4**).

1 Using the wet-on-wet technique you can create the most attractive colour flows.

2 The wet-on-wet technique is well suited for combination with the outliner technique.

3 After drying you can wash out the colour using thinner or water.

4 The wash-out technique is very good for creating abstract patterns.

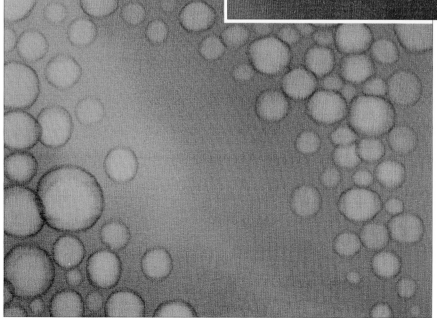

3

A blue flow

Using the wet-on-wet technique, painting gentle flowing colour transitions is straightforward. On the following pages we shall show you a few basic exercises. Although they may look very simple, do not bypass these. Only through practical application will you acquire a feeling for the correct way to paint. You will thus avoid errors when painting your own designs later on.

MATERIALS
Silk: 30 × 30 cm (12 × 12 in) or 20 × 20 cm (8 × 8 in) habutai silk or crêpe de Chine
Colour: dark blue
Brushes: flat sable brush no 18 or sable brush no 8
Technique: watercolour (wet-on-wet) technique

Use the flat brush to apply water evenly on to the silk. No pools of water should form. If they do, remove the excess using a paper handkerchief or kitchen towel. Dip the brush into the dark blue and apply the colour, starting at the bottom, in even, parallel, horizontal brushstrokes roughly as far as the centre of the surface. Do not allow the silk to dry out. It must remain damp across its entire surface. Then wash out the brush a little, leaving a small amount of colour on the brush. Use

that to paint the rest of the area.

Next, use a water-soaked brush to go over the picture, working from the bottom to the top as before, and blend in the colour transitions.

If you want to increase the contrast in the colour runs, spread some more dark blue, working upwards from the bottom, as far as the middle of the picture and massage the colours from the bottom to the top (**1**) swiftly.

The colour flow from dark to light is now complete. Where the silk is taut, unwanted stripes of colour may appear. Therefore, make sure that the silk is not too tightly stretched, or be generous when you calculate the frame size (**2**).

Tip: If the colour application becomes too heavy, you can lessen it

with water and wipe away excess colour using a paper handkerchief. You can remove small, uneven areas in the colour flow by making the still damp silk wet and by using a brush to blend the colours gently into one another. When you do this you must work quickly across the entire area otherwise edge marks may appear where the colour dries again. Such marks cannot be removed.

1

2

A red-yellow flow

Dampen the silk with water and paint a full-tone red, in horizontal parallel brushstrokes, from the bottom upwards across one-third of the picture. Undiluted colour is known as full-tone.

Wash out the brush and work the edge of the area of colour with water. Then paint a full-tone yellow in the upper third of the picture, working from the top downwards, and again work the edge of the area of colour with water. It is important that you leave a white strip between the two colours so that you can gently draw them into one another. Later the strength of the colour flow will depend on the width of the white strip.

Next, use a watercolour brush to spread the yellow and red into the white area until you have a gentle colour transition. Here, too, you should work with horizontal/parallel brushstrokes. If you want to increase the contrast, pull in more colour from above and below.

It is important that the silk is damp while you are carrying out this procedure (**3**).

You have now created a gentle colour flow (**4**).

MATERIALS
Silk: 30 × 30 cm (12 × 12 in) or 20 × 20 cm (8 × 8 in) habutai silk or crêpe de Chine
Colours: red and yellow
Brushes: flat sable brush no 18 or sable brush no 8
Technique: watercolour (wet-on-wet) technique

Tips: Remember to wash out the brushes between the individual colour stages.

Have a watercolour brush at the ready so that you can keep the silk damp.

Work evenly but rapidly. When painting wet-on-wet the colours must not be allowed to dry while you are still painting.

Test various colour flows on different silks.

When painting colour flows you should use two water jars, one in which you wash out your brushes, and one with clear water for massaging the colours.

Painting larger areas wet-on-wet is considerably more difficult than painting smaller areas. Therefore, test this technique as often as possible on small pieces of silk before attempting to apply it to large pieces, such as shawls or a scarf with a rainbow design.

Use an appropriate broad brush for large areas. Make sure that you always have sufficient mixed colour at the ready.

3

4

PAINTING ON DAMP AND DRY SURFACES

Painting on damp surfaces

You can easily test the effects of painting on damp and dry surfaces – so experiment a little.

Dampen the silk using water and – with a brush – apply dots of differing sizes on to the damp surface. The colour spreads in all directions, but not evenly. On damp silk it flows very obviously in the direction of the thread, particularly the warp. Water in the silk increases the drying time (**1**).

The dots are now dry. Slight edge marks have formed (**2**).

Painting on dry surfaces

Apply dots of colour to a piece of dry silk. Here the colour does not spread out as much as it does on damp silk. It does, however, flow much more evenly in all directions (**3**).

On drier silk the dots and their edges are more even than those on wet silk because the colour does not run as quickly (**4**).

Try these exercises on different kinds of silk. Each type of fabric has its own specific effect on the flow characteristics of the colour. Colour spreads more quickly on thinner fabrics.

MATERIALS
Silk: 30 × 30 cm (12 × 12 in) or 20 × 20 cm (8 × 8 in) crêpe de Chine or habutai silk
Colours: iron-fixable and steam-fixable colours
Brushes: sable brush no 8 or 9
Technique: watercolour technique

You can control the flow of the colours with a hair dryer (see page 72) and thus influence the colour runs. In these exercises, in addition to the flow characteristics of the colours, you will also notice that the colours appear slightly darker when wet than once dry.

So that you do not get any unexpected results later, before you begin painting, carry out a colour drop test (see page 12) on a small piece of silk and dry the colour using a hair dryer. The silk on which you carry out the test and the silk on which you intend to paint should be the same material. You can now make a good assessment of the colour effect. The colours may be further intensified by the fixing process.

1

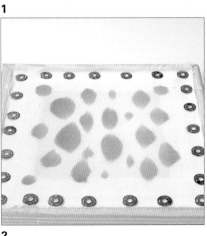

2

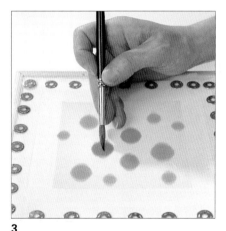

3

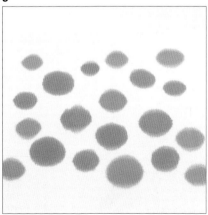

4

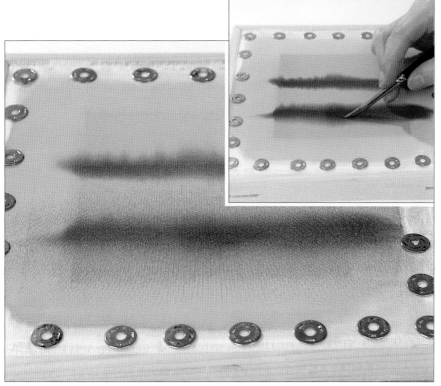

5 and 6

7

In the examples on this page the silk had already been painted yellow. Here too the effect of the colour that you apply to the yellow background will depend on whether or not the background is dry or wet.

Painting on damp surfaces
Paint an even yellow tone on to the silk and then paint two red parallel stripes on the area of colour that is still damp (**5**).

The colours have dried. The colour stripes have gently merged at the edges (**6**).

This wet-on-wet painting effect is very good for designs with a strong atmospheric character, such as mists or water surfaces. A good example of this is the picture 'At Sea' (page 128).

Painting on dry surfaces
This is the same exercise, but here the red stripes were not added until the background had completely dried. Unlike when painting on a wet background, the colour stripes have spread only a little, the edges are more distinct and the red is more intense. The reason for this is that the colour does not spread as much on a dry background as on a damp one. Thus the thinning effect of the water is also lost (**7**).

As you can see, it is possible to obtain relatively clear contours, even without outliners, if you paint on dry backgrounds. Therefore the drier your paintbrush, the more control you will have over the flow of the colour.

You can also strongly influence the flow of the colours by first applying a primer to the silk (see page 76).

THINNING TECHNIQUE

Painting with colour, water and alcohol

Thinning can have a considerable influence on the characteristics of colours. The traditional steam-fixable colours are thinned using a mixture of alcohol and water. This dilutes the colour and improves its flow qualities on the silk.

Alcohol has a stronger effect on the colour than water; it actually encourages the colour to penetrate the material. It does, however, evaporate relatively quickly.

Water thins colours, enabling them to spread better across the material. Water dries relatively slowly, so you can control the flow and drying capacities of the silk painting colours according to the amounts of water and alcohol you mix together. Thinner is available commercially ready mixed. You can also make it up yourself by mixing industrial alcohol, available from chemists, and distilled water. If you want the colour to flow well and to dry slowly, increase the proportion of water, making a solution that is one part alcohol and three parts water. This will make applying the colours easy. If you want the colours to dry quickly, increase the proportion of alcohol, making a solution of three parts alcohol to one part water, for example. Iron-fixable colours may only be thinned using water.

Washing out colours

Using alcohol and water you can, to a certain extent, wash out colours or lighten shades that are too dark. You can also use alcohol and water in this way to remove some areas of colour almost entirely, if you have made a mistake or if you want to create a light area. You can work such areas with water and thinner. This dissolves the colour and drives it outwards.

For traditional silk painting colours, use a mixture of alcohol and water. The greater the proportion of alcohol, the stronger the thinning effect will be.

Iron-fixable colours should be washed out with water only. The washing-out effect is at its most intense on dry silk. If the silk is damp, the lightening effect is limited. On these pages we show you how you

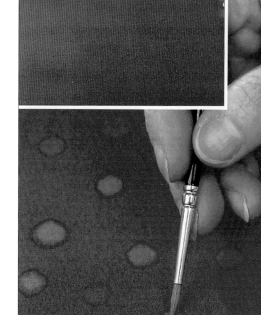

1 and 2

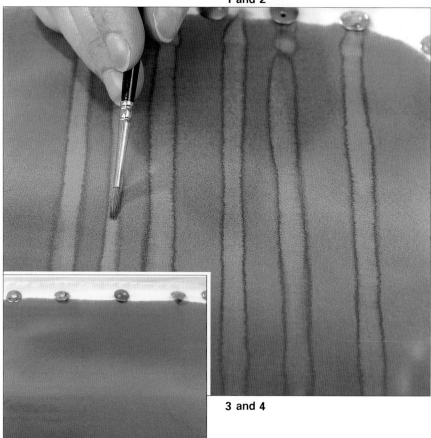

3 and 4

can wash out areas after they have been painted.

Exercise 1

Paint an area of even red on to the silk. Do not thin the colour very much; instead, apply it as a full tone. This will make the washing-out effect all the more intensive (**1**).

Use a thinner or water to wash out a few dots from the red area. Do not take up too much water or thinner into the brush as this may cause the dot to spread out of control. Wipe the brush on a paper handkerchief, leaving only a small amount of liquid in the brush. Then briefly dab the red area with the tip of the brush, and take the brush off the surface immediately. You will now see how the water or thinner pushes the colour in front of it. Alcohol lightens the colour more than water. Where the effect comes to an end, a dark edge is formed. The more you wash

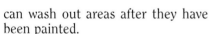

5

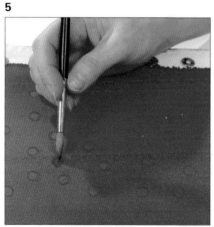

6

7

out this particular area, the darker the edge becomes. In picture 2 the two points just to the left of the one being worked on have been washed out only once. If the drying time is longer, in other words if the water content is greater, a more jagged edge forms. If on the other hand you use a greater alcohol content when washing out, the edge formed is sharp and straight. You can increase this effect by using a hair dryer (**2**).

In pictures 5, 6 and 7 you can see how the dots change as a result of washing out if you hold the brush for too long on the silk and if you wash out using too much water or thinner in the brush.

Exercise 2

Paint blue-green wet-on-wet (**3**).

Wash out some parallel stripes. Draw the lines rapidly, applying brush pressure as evenly as possible. If the pressure is uneven, the amount of water and thinner released will also be uneven which in turn will cause the width of the stripes to vary. Small irregularities will not matter, however. In fact, quite the opposite; they enliven your silk painting. If you do not draw your stripes in one stroke, thickening may occur at the point where you restart the stripe (**4**).

MATERIALS

Silk: 30 × 30 cm (12 × 12 in) or 20 × 20 cm (8 × 8 in) crêpe de Chine or habutai silk
Colours: steam-fixable or iron-fixable colours
Brush: sable brush no 8
Technique: thinning technique

Painting with a hair dryer

A hair dryer is an important tool in silk painting. It makes painting on damp silk much easier. As long as the silk is damp you can use the warm stream of air from the dryer to influence shapes, edges and highlights that are still changing.

If you have achieved the desired effect with your painting or washing out, stop the changing process by using the hair dryer to dry the appropriate place quickly. The best way to do this is to hold the dryer in your left hand and paint or wash out with your right. (If you are left-handed, hold the dryer in your right hand.)

The paintings on these two pages were painted using a combination of the wet-on-wet technique and the thinning technique and then dried with a hair dryer.

Tips: Select a warm, gentle air stream. It should be neither too hot nor too strong.

Gently fan the air stream backwards and forwards across the silk, particularly if you are using the hair dryer to dry colours or primers. Do not hold the dryer for too long over one place as this could cause edge marks to form. A dryer is a particularly useful tool if you are washing out clear shapes from an area of colour. Wash out the shape several times using just a little thinner, and dry the area quickly using the hair dryer. This will avoid uncontrolled changes in the areas being washed out.

You will create straight colour edges when working with colour, water or thinner if you immediately use the hair dryer.

If you are trying to obtain a more diffuse edge, the colour or liquid must first be allowed to run. Then dry the area using the hair dryer. From the pictures on these two pages you can see that clear contour lines can be achieved using the dryer without having to use outliner.

Coloured Stripe Pattern

Paint several lines in different colours, wet-on-wet, next to one another and dry them using the hair dryer. Wash out the colour stripes using thinner in such a way that the edges of the stripes meet. Repeat this process a couple more times until you have achieved the desired effect. Wait until jagged indentations form before drying your picture using the hair dryer.

The coloured stripes should be dried thoroughly with the dryer before you wash out the adjacent stripes, otherwise the edges may flow into one another (**1**).

Evening Mood by the Lake

Before you begin painting, mix up the following colour shades: for the sky you will need a light blue, a gentle blue-violet, a soft pale blue-pink and a light pink shade; for the water mix up various colder and warmer blue shades.

Dampen the silk thoroughly using water and a brush, and paint, wet-on-wet, the sky in the given colour shades. Leave some white spaces. From below paint a light turquoise into the colour area that is still wet, and allow it to merge into the sky. Give the wet, turquoise area a bit of

1

2

interest by adding a few stripes of different blues, and then fade the edges. Next, dry the silk with a hair dryer.

Wash out the stripes using thinner. So that you do not get any jagged edges, quickly dry the stripes using the dryer. You will have gentle colour transitions after just a few washings-out.

To strengthen the wave effect you can paint a few more colour shades, which you thin several times, next to the blue stripes (**2** and **3**).

Little Mountain Landscape
Mix up some colours of your choice; paint, wet-on-wet, the sky and the mountains and dry the picture with a hair dryer. Wash out the chain of mountains using thinner and immediately fix the lines that form as a result with the hair dryer. Wash out several times so that slightly sharper contour lines are formed (**4**).

Given the method of the wet-on-wet silk painting technique and the many washings-out, it is not possible to recreate the pictures on these pages exactly. But that does not matter. The purpose of these exercises is to get you used to working with the technique and to carry out lots of experimentation. That way you will quickly find the style that suits you best.

MATERIALS
Silk: 30 × 30 cm (12 × 12 in) habutai silk
Colours: steam-fixable silk painting colours
Brush: sable brush no 8
Technique: watercolour (wet-on-wet) technique and thinning technique

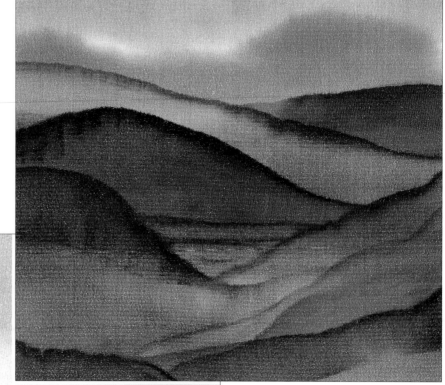

4

3

Painting with colour, thinner and a hair dryer

Designing and painting patterns is an enjoyable and inventive pastime, so you should view the suggestions on these pages only as stimulation for your own designs.

Try out all the watercolour techniques: wet-on-wet, washing out, and painting with a hair dryer. Patterns and shapes are particularly well suited to these because they are not based on a strict motif. And you do not need to worry about mistakes. In fact, quite the opposite is true; perhaps a mistake will lead you to a new effect.

Tip: Paint your patterns on different silk fabrics and use different types of brush. This is the best way to get to know your working materials.

Each time you carry out an exercise, note down the individual working steps and the brushes and silk you used. This will make it easier for you to reproduce the same effects at a later date.

Row Pattern

For this pattern the white of the silk is incorporated in the effect. Paint your pattern on to the dry silk and hold the individual lines immediately using the hair dryer. Next, wash out parts of the pattern using water, and then use the dryer where necessary (**1**).

Veil Pattern

Wet-on-wet, paint a pastel flow on to the silk and paint the initial shapes on to the area that is still damp.

1

Lighten these shapes using water and then dry them with the hair dryer. Paint some more patterns on to the now dry background, and keep them in place by drying them with the hair dryer; wash out some of them again.

For the final painting step, mix a scumble using water or thinner and a little grey. You will have to stir the mixture thoroughly.

Use a wide brush to draw stripes of scumble across the pattern. Leave a gap between each stripe.

Work quickly, and immediately dry the individual scumble stripes with the hair dryer. This creates a very attractive effect. The scumble stripes lie like a delicate veil draped across the pattern. At some points the pattern is feint and gauzy; at others, it is much stronger and more distinct (**2**).

MATERIALS
Silk: 30 × 40 cm (12 × 16 in) habutai silk
Colours: steam-fixable silk painting colours
Brush: sable brush no 8
Technique: watercolour (wet-on-wet) technique and thinning technique

2

PRIMERS

Painting on safe ground

The brush glides freely across the silk. Fine lines, gentle strokes and clear shapes flow from the brush head and the colour does not run! What is the secret? You prime the surface before applying the colour. Then you can paint even the tiniest of details on to the silk using a brush.

The primer stops colours running. This makes it possible to paint precise contours without the use of outliner lines. If, however, the colour continues to run, apply a second coat of primer. As soon as the primer has dried you can paint very fine detail with a brush – like the motifs or free-form shapes and patterns on these two pages.

Ready-mixed primers are produced by various manufacturers and are available commercially. Follow the instructions carefully. Our patterns were painted using Deka Silk and Deka primer (**1**).

Carry out a test before you prime and paint your design.

On primed silk you can also use the salt technique or wash out the colours with thinner.

The patterns are painted on to dry primers using steam-fixable colours (**2**).

Salt primer

(No illustration shown) Dissolve 250 g (8 oz) of cooking salt into 1 litre (2 pints) of water. Stir the solution well, ensuring that all the salt dissolves, then leave it to stand for a while. Next, pour the solution through a coffee filter paper so that no sediment remains in the primer. Apply the solution to the silk using a brush. The way in which the primer dries will affect its characteristics. If allowed to dry slowly, large salt crystals will form. These give rise to coarse textures in the painting. If you dry the primer quickly using a hair dryer, small crystals form which scatter more delicately across the silk. This means that you can paint filigree shapes on to the primer.

Before you start to paint, test to see how colours react to the salt primer.

One characteristic of salt is that it breaks down secondary colours into their original components (see also Salt technique, page 58). Salt primers form a good base for working with alcohol.

Tip: You do not have to apply the primer to the silk in its white state. You may instead like to apply a background of soft pastel shades and then prime the silk after the background has dried. You can then paint your design on to the primer without it bleeding into the background.

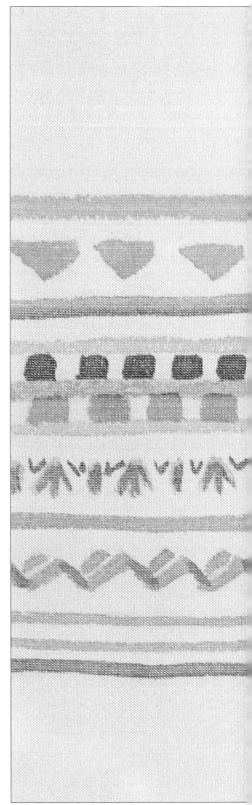

Patterns painted using Deka Silk and Deka primer

1

2

JAPANESE LANDSCAPE

A small, dreamy bay invitingly beckons you to linger a while. A tree bends over the blue-green water of the lake, creating an attractive contrast to the peaceful background.

This small, meditative landscape is painted wet-on-wet. By employing primers (see page 76) you can paint very fine details without having to use outliner. You can test out many of the watercolour techniques while painting this picture.

MATERIALS

Silk: 30 × 30 cm (12 × 12 in) crêpe de Chine

Colours: steam-fixable silk painting colours

Top row of colour chart: lemon, turquoise

Middle row of colour chart: pea green, brilliant blue

Bottom row of colour chart: brown olive green mixed using may green, lemon and a little rhodamine; blue-green mixed using may green and a little brilliant blue

Brushes: two sable brushes, no 6 or no 8, one for colours and one for water; one no 18 sable flat brush

Primer: Deka primer

Technique: watercolour technique

Colour sketch
Before you begin the actual painting, use coloured pencils to draw a colour draft. This will enable you to see whether or not the colours you have chosen go well together (**1**).

Painting blue shades
Before you begin painting, mix up the following colour shades on a palette: use water to thin down turquoise to a very light pastel shade, and brilliant blue down to two pastel shades, one lighter and the other somewhat darker.

Dampen the silk by applying water to it. Allow the surface to dry a little. When you paint, no water should be lying on the silk.

Paint the surface of the lake using the turquoise pastel tone. In a few places allow the white of the silk to shimmer through. This makes the water surface more lively. Always avoid painting a single-tone water surface – it looks unnatural.

Paint the mountains using the pastel tones mixed from the brilliant blue. As the mountains have to retain their white snowtops, use a watercolour brush to work against the colour, ensuring that the blue does not run into the white areas. The brush should not be too wet (**2**).

1

2

Painting yellow shades

You will need a full-tone lemon and two mixtures: one pastel tone mixed from lemon and a little water; and a warmer yellow mixed from yellow and a little red.

Use these three yellow shades to paint in the still-damp sky area. Here too you should allow white areas to shimmer through. Wash the yellow tones, wet-on-wet, into one another. Allow the yellow to run gently towards the mountains.

If the colour actually runs into the mountains, draw the yellow colour upwards away from the mountains using a watercolour brush that is not too wet. Then dry the picture with a hair dryer (**3**).

Applying the primer

Apply Deka primer evenly to the silk using a flat brush or a sable no 6 or no 8. The primer should be well stirred before it is applied (**4**).

Painting rocks

Paint the rocks using the pastel shades made from the brilliant blue. The brush should be as dry as possible. So that the rocks appear three-dimensional, leave some light areas and draw the brilliant blue pastel shades into the white areas using the watercolour brush.

If you feel that the primer is not adequately controlling the flow of your colours, apply a second coat of primer (**5**).

Applying blue shadows to the mountains

Make the brilliant blue shade that you used for the mountains slightly darker. You can also add a little red to it. This will make the shade a little warmer.

Using a brush that is as dry as possible, paint shadows in the mountains. In so doing, make sure that the shadows give the mountains structure. To do this they must closely follow the shape of the mountains. Light and dark shades make the mountains three-dimensional (**6**).

3

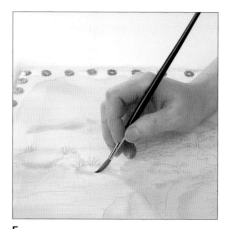

5

4

6

1 The colour sketch clearly shows the intended effect of the completed picture.

2 Start with the blue shades and paint the lake and the mountains.

3 Use different shades of yellow to create the sunny sky.

4 Apply the primer so that the colours applied thereafter do not run.

5 Blue areas and areas of bright light lend the rocks their shape.

6 The mountain shadows are also applied in blue.

Painting green hills

For the chain of hills reaching down to the water, mix the following two green shades on your palette: and a mixture of may green diluted with water; and a mixture of may green, water and a little lemon. The latter is a warmer tone. Apply the green shades to the hills and use a water-colour brush to wash the colours into one another. These areas should also be made three-dimensional by interspersing the green shades with lighter and darker areas. Then dry the picture using a hair dryer (**7**).

Painting shadows under the rocks

Mix up two blue shades: a dark brilliant blue and a dark blue-green, using brilliant blue and may green.

Paint delicate shadows under the rocks using as dry a brush tip as possible. In so doing make sure that the shadows beneath the rocks in the foreground are slightly darker. This follows the rule that colours in the foreground of a picture should be stronger and darker than those in the background. Dark colours force their way forward while lighter colours recede and add perspective (see A Lesson in Colour beginning on page 85). On the other hand, the colour of the stones should not be too dark as this may destroy the picture's brightness. A clear balance has to be struck (**8**).

7

8

9

10

Grasses and shrubs

To paint the grass and bushes, mix together three colour shades: a medium may green and two different light olive greens mixed from may green, lemon and a little red. When painting the plants, always apply the colour from the bottom moving upwards. Use lively, upward brushstrokes. This gives the grass a natural appearance.

First apply the lighter shades to the grass and then dry the colour using a hair dryer. Give the grass contours using darker green shades. Also use the darker green tones to shade the chain of hills that you have already painted in green. This will enliven the surface (**9**).

The tree

Mix up a dark and a light blue-green using brilliant blue and may green; also mix up a brown olive green using may green, lemon and red.

Here, too, you should work with a dry brush. Paint the trunk and the branches using the brown olive shade. Paint the needles blue-green. Once again, the brush movements should be outwards towards the tips of the needles. The tree in the foreground has a strong accentuation. The light-coloured background recedes behind the strong colours of the tree. This not only gives the painting depth; it also gives it interest as a result of the tonal contrast (**10**).

7 For the chain of hills mix together light green shades using diluted may green and lemon.

8 Using a dry brush, paint shadows under the rocks.

9 Paint the clumps of grass from their base upwards, just as the plants actually grow.

10 The dark green shades of the tree emphasise the foreground.

Reflections in the water

Mix two dark colour shades using turquoise and brilliant blue and paint a few reflections in the water. For example, you can reflect the mountains in the background, inverted as they would be in a mirror. Do not be too exact or you will lose the effect of the water's surface. The result should be a mixture of waves and slightly distorted reflections. The waves are painted as horizontal parallel lines. This gives the impression of a calm but not glassy lake (**11**).

The finished picture

You picture is still very delicate because it has not yet been fixed. One single drop of water could destroy everything! Therefore, remove the painting from the frame immediately and store it carefully until you are ready to fix it (**12**).

Just a few colour shades have created a miniature magical landscape. The many gentle colour flows create attractive light and shadow effects. They are painted wet-on-wet and on primer. Thus the watercolour technique allows you to create shapes and colours on the silk very freely using a brush. At the same time you can employ this technique to paint clear contours. The result is a charming mixture of gentle colour transitions, precise outlines and delicate textures. The colours become far more attractive after fixing and cleaning (**13**).

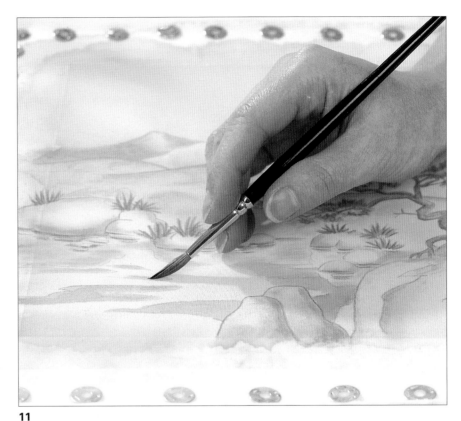

11

11 Parallel reflections indicate small waves.

12 The final brushstroke has been made. All that is left to do is fix the silk painting.

13 The completed picture. An idyllic landscape has been created on the silk.

12

The world of colours

Sun yellow, sky blue and fire red – from these clear, elementary colours an infinite number of new colour shades can be mixed, ranging from a gentle green to a brilliant orange. Colours give out signals; they excite us or calm us. In this chapter you will learn a few basic rules about what effects colours have and how they influence one another.

PRIMARY AND SECONDARY

Mixing well is half the battle

The world of colours is determined by the three primary colours – red, yellow and blue. You can mix every other colour shade from these three colours.

Red and yellow make orange, blue and yellow make green, blue and red make violet. Also compare the colours in the middle of the colour wheel on page 87 with those on the colour scale on the right-hand side of this page.

You can easily try these mixtures for yourself in each case by painting two of the primary colours, wet-on-wet beside one another, on a piece of damp silk and allowing them to merge in the middle. You will see that the colours change and a large number of colour mixtures are created depending on the amount of each primary colour used. In principle, for silk painting you need buy only the three primary colours.

Usually these are called the primary colours, but some manufacturers refer to them as the euro-colours. It does make silk painting much easier, however, if you also buy a few of your favourite colours ready mixed. It is very difficult to recreate a precise colour shade a second time. It is therefore advisable, before painting large items such as scarves or shawls, to mix up enough colour so that you do not run out during painting.

You can mix smaller quantities of colour in a porcelain or plastic colour palette; larger quantities can be mixed in a jar. Collect jars with screw-top lids in which you can then store any unused colour.

Please note that when mixing colours, light colours such as yellow do not have as strong an influence on dark colours as vice versa. To mix a medium orange, for example, you will need much more yellow than red. Therefore, when you start to mix up colours, always begin with the light colour to which you then carefully add the dark colour until you have the desired shade.

To mix precise silk painting colours, use a pipette. This allows you to count exactly how many colour drops are used (eg two drops of red plus five drops of yellow) and thus to record just how you obtained the shade. Before changing colour, make sure that the pipette is washed out thoroughly with water – just as you do with your brushes. The same also applies when you have finished using the pipette. If it is not washed out thoroughly, colour sediment will build up which can then interfere with colour mixes that you make at a later stage. Paint each new colour mix on to silk and record the mixture proportions of the individual colour shades. In this way you can build up an attractive colour archive to which you can refer for future mixes.

A colour chart is also very helpful. This gives you a good overview of your most important colour mixtures. Creating a colour chart is explained on page 88.

To mix small quantities of colour by eye on the colour palette, use a brush. You can add black to darken

Red

Yellow

Blue

Red – Orange – Yellow

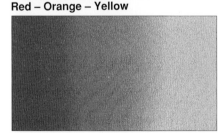

Blue – Green – Yellow

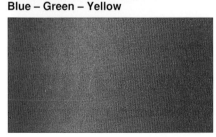

Blue – Lilac – Red

the colour, and thinner to lighten it. Here too the effect can be calculated if, before painting, you test the effect of darkening and lightening the main colours. To do this, invest in what is known as a colour flute (see page 90).

The colour wheel

The colour wheel, created by the Bauhaus painter Johannes Itten, is a useful tool when it comes to mixing colours. The three primary colours yellow, red and blue lie inside the wheel, as do their related secondary colours orange, violet and green.

In the outer wheel you can see a total of twelve colours all of which are derived from the primary colours. A colour lying between two other colours is mixed using those colours.

Colours lying directly opposite one another on the colour wheel are called complementary colours. Yellow and violet, blue and orange, and red and green respectively are complementary colours. If complementary colours are mixed together the result is a grey colour shade.

Brown shades are created by mixing together the three primary colours yellow, red and blue.

Left: The primary colours red, yellow and blue at the top of the colour ladder were painted, in pairs and wet on wet, on to silk. The colours were therefore mixed on the silk itself. This creates attractive, smooth colour runs and infinite mixtures of colour. In the run between red and yellow, orange dominates; in the blue and yellow run, green has the strongest effect; and in the blue and red run purple is particularly noticeable.
Using your primary colours, paint similar runs on to silk; you will notice immediately how your colours mix.

Right: Johannes Itten's colour wheel gives you a good overview of which colours to use to create the different colour mixes.

MIXING COLOURS

The colour chart

Mixing colours is a great art, particularly if you have very definite ideas about the colour nuances and effects you wish to achieve.

You should therefore make a colour chart for yourself, showing the most important secondary colours. Write down how much of each primary colour you used to create various intermediate shades so that you are able to remix them later.

Colour chart 1

Using outliner, draw a three- by seven-block grid on to the silk and leave it to dry. In each of the three horizontal rows, two primary colours will be mixed to create five different intermediate shades.

In the top row, mix the primary colours yellow and blue. Paint the extreme left block full-tone blue, and the extreme right block full-tone yellow. Then, on your colour palette, add a little blue to the primary colour yellow and paint the resultant colour into the second block from the right.

Repeat this process four more times, each time adding more and more blue to the yellow, until the mixture approaches the full-tone blue on the left.

In the same way, paint the middle row using the primary colours yellow and red; and paint the bottom row using the primary colours red and blue. In each case you create five colour mixes.

After drying, fix the colours and clean the silk. Only now can you see the true colour effect of the primary and secondary colours and the shades they will create later in your silk paintings.

Colour chart 2

For this chart the colours will be mixed in the same proportions as for colour chart 1 described above.

The only difference is that this time thinner is added to the painted and dried colour fields. This will cause the colours to be forced to the edge towards the outliner lines. There the colours become somewhat darker. In the middle of the blocks, the colours are lighter.

Before you start to paint, make a colour sketch using coloured pencils. Compare the colours in the sketch with those on your colour chart. Now you can select the appropriate colours and adjust the mixes until you have the required colour shades.

For painting, mix your colours in a colour palette or in jars. You can determine the amounts very precisely using a pipette – in other

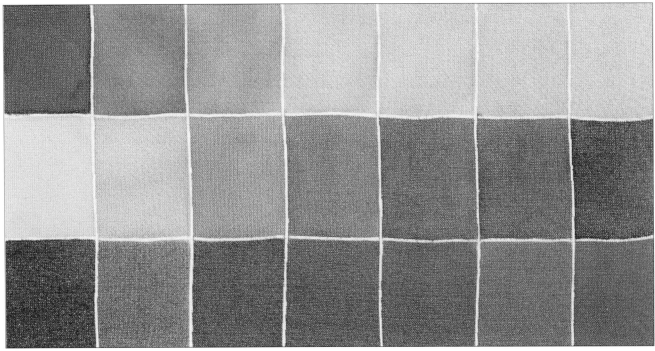

1

words, you can create very exact mixtures.

You can mix the colours directly on the silk. To do this the silk must be wet. Paint the colours in parallel brushstrokes from the left and the right into the middle of the silk, using the wet-on-wet technique. A flowing colour transition is created made up of intermediate shades merging gently into one another. When you are painting, think about the emotional effect, as well as the optical impression, of the colours you are using. A calm blue has a different effect to that of a sensuous red. Colours not only express mood, they also stimulate associations: moss green, violet-purple and deer brown are reminiscent of a wood and nature. Irish green, arctic blue and sahara yellow are colours that provoke dreams of faraway places. Colours fire our imaginations. They

can give us a sense of well-being or discomfiture; they can make us calm or aggressive.

The interplay between the colour shades you use is vital in your pictures. Whether you paint tone-on-tone or in stark contrasts, with a little experience you will soon ascertain which colours go together. The rules governing this are explained in this chapter. You will also be shown a few exercises that you really should carry out. Hands-on experience with the brush and colours is just as important as theoretical knowledge about how colours work.

Everything depends on putting together the correct colours. This will determine the strength of expression in your picture. Everything is possible – from gaudy, vivid colour combinations giving an impression of distance, to light, clear moods full of harmony. Give it a try! The lesson

in colours will help you to put into practice the colour and picture ideas you have.

MATERIALS

Silk: habutai silk (the size will depend on the size of the boxes in the grid)

Colours: steam-fixable silk painting colours: the primary colours yellow, red and blue

Outliner: spirit-based outliner

Technique: outliner technique

1 Colour chart 1
2 Colour chart 2

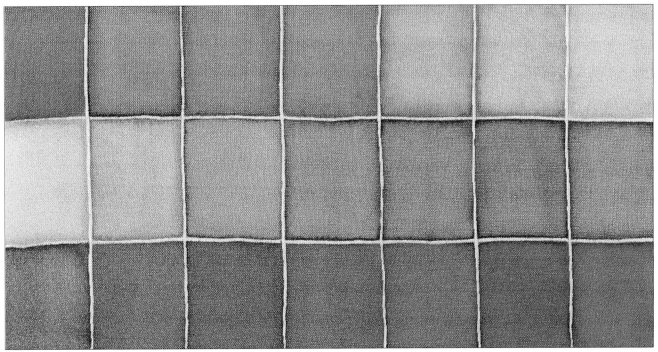

The colour flute from dark to light

Many of the colour shades can be made by darkening or lightening the primary or secondary colours.

Lightening and darkening

To lighten a colour, add water or thinner depending on the product (**2**).

The traditional silk painting colours are thinned using a mixture of water and alcohol. You can, however, thin these colours using water only. This means that they stay damp for longer during painting, which is particularly convenient if you are painting large areas. A further effect is that edge marks do not form so quickly.

In traditional silk painting you do not use white for lightening. The transparent silk painting colours, when used with the appropriate thinner, allow the white of the silk to shine through and thus create a lighter effect.

In silk painting, areas that need to be white should not be painted (see page 94). Something called 'mix white' does exist for certain iron-fixable colours, such as Deka-Silk.

The more black you add to your colours, the darker they become (**3**).

Colour flute

Darkening and lightening colours looks simpler than it actually is. Black, in particular, can soon make your colours appear sombre. Therefore, make up a colour flute of the most important colours and mark on it how certain colours react to darkening and lightening. In principle a colour flute is nothing more than a colour chart (see page 88). Using outliner, paint a seven- by seven-block grid on to a piece of silk and leave it to dry. In the top row paint pairs, in full tone, of the primary colours blue, red and yellow and then use the final box for black.

Using thinner or water, lighten each colour in six stages, painting down one column for each colour, each box containing a shade lighter than the last.

Then, in the same way, paint the respective adjacent rows, this time adding more and more black to the primary colours so that each box contains a shade darker than the last one. This gives you a good overview of the effect of darkening and lightening colours. Here too you should use the pipette and write down each time the amount of colour and black or colour and thinner or water used. Then, later, you will be able to use your colour flute and records quickly to remix the colour shades you need (**1**).

Colour games

Using outliner, create a grid and experiment. For example, mix the primary colour blue with other colours and lighten the colours or darken them. Paint the most attractive colours on to the grid. Try out your colours.

Place lots of colours next to each

1

2

3

other and observe the effect. In this way not only will you be able to create a wide variety of colour moods, you will at the same time also paint an attractive colour mosaic that may form a very expressive composition in its own right. You will quickly learn which colours harmonise well and which strengthen or suppress one another. Also read the section entitled 'Painting Contrasts' on page 92 (**4**).

Tip: Many attractive colours can also be mixed using grey.

MATERIALS
Silk: habutai silk (the size will depend on the size of the boxes in the grid)
Colours: steam-fixable silk painting colours: blue, red, yellow and black
Outliner: spirit-based outliner
Technique: outliner-technique

1 Colour flute
Lightening and darkening changes the primary colours dramatically.

2 Lightening
You can lighten the colours using a little water or thinner.

3 Darkening
You darken the colours using black.

4 Colour games
You can paint a colour mosaic using darkened or lightened primary and secondary colours.

4

PAINTING CONTRASTS

Contrasts

The effect a picture has is the result of the contrasts within it. A picture painted in graduated blues rather than the same brightness value. You can use the warm-cold contrast to create strong impressions of depth. Warm colours force their way, optically, into the foreground while cold blue shades appear to recede (see The World of Colours beginning on page 86).

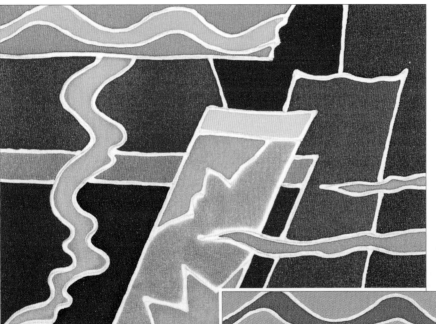

1

lacks contrast. A red accent, however, enlivens the blue which then begins to shine. There are various contrasts which increase the intensity of the colours.

The warm-cold contrast

A hot red makes cold blue look even colder. Warm colours increase the effect of cold colours and vice versa. They lie directly opposite each other on the colour wheel. The more yellow a colour contains, the warmer its effect. The greater its blue content, the colder the effect. The warm-cold contrast is greatest if the colours used have

The complementary contrast

The complementary colours are: red and green; blue and orange; yellow and violet. Each pair of colours are opposite each other on the colour wheel. An interesting phenomenon should be noted where complementary colours are concerned: the eye automatically creates the complementary colour of any colour it sees. Thus, a grey lying next to a red has a slightly green appearance. By the same token, a grey lying next to a green has a reddish tint. So complementary colours strengthen one another and create harmony.

The light-dark contrast

The contrast between light and dark colours can give pictures a strong

2

three-dimensional effect because you are in fact using pale colours to create light and darker shades to create shadow. Pictures are given depth by the fact that dark colours, just like warm colours, appear to move to the foreground.

The bright–dull contrast

Broken colours make pure colours shine. Colours are broken when a complementary colour is added to them.

The quantity contrast

Each colour has its own strength of expression. Some are stronger – such as yellow and orange – and some are weaker – blue and violet for example. In order to create a picture in which the colours are well balanced, take the colour strength into account and give the weaker colours a little more space than you give to the stronger colours. You may like to think about this if you feel that your colour composition is not yet quite right. Often the reason for this is that the quantity contrast is not in balance.

MATERIALS
Silk: 30 × 24 cm (12 × 9½ in) habutai silk
Colours: steam-fixable silk painting colours

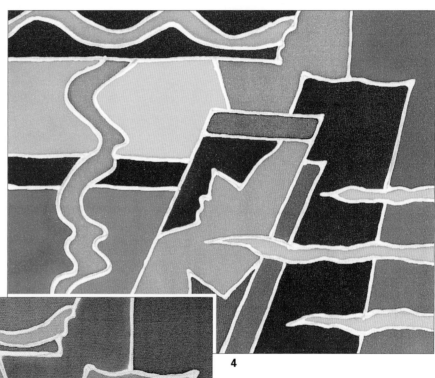

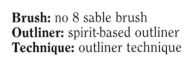

4

Brush: no 8 sable brush
Outliner: spirit-based outliner
Technique: outliner technique

1 The warm colours are the yellow-red shades, ranging from red-mauve through orange to yellow.

2 The cold colours are green, blue and violet.

3 Cold colours become warmer if yellow is added to them.

4 Complementary colours mutually strengthen one another. They create effects ranging from the strong and bold to vivid shimmers.

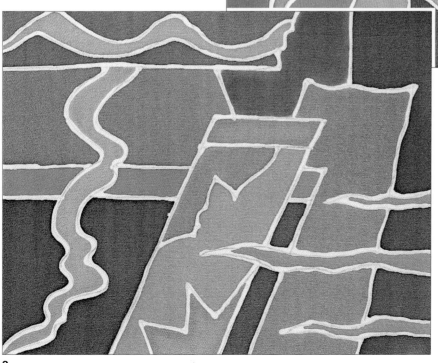

3

PAINTING WITHOUT WHITE

Using the white of the silk

The range of colours for silk painting is enormous, but one colour is missing: white. The silk to which you apply the colours is itself white. The basic white of the silk is, therefore, the white used in silk painting. Therefore, you must never paint over areas in a picture that are to appear white. These areas stay white from the outset.

The reason for this is simple: silk painting colours do not cover areas opaquely, they allow light to shine through the colour, just like watercolours. Therefore, overpainting will only darken colour shades, not lighten them.

It is true that a mix-white was de-

1

2

veloped for iron-fixable colours (Deka, for example, developed just such a white). But as it is alien to silk painting it has not been used for the designs in this book. It is possible to lighten colour areas up to a certain point by washing them out with water or thinner (see 'Washing-out Technique' on page 70). The transparent silk painting colours let the white of the silk shine through.

The more you thin the colours the more the white of the silk becomes visible and the lighter the effect of the colours (see Colour Flute on page 90).

Planning in advance

Because, in principle, overpainting merely darkens the colours and will not lighten them, you must begin each silk painting with the lightest colour and then, step by step, apply even darker shades around or over the areas of light colour. This means that you need to plan in advance in precisely what order you will paint the colours in your design. If you use a prepared colour sketch, however, the process should not be too difficult.

Tips: Silk painting white does not exist. The white in silk painting is the white of the silk itself.

All those areas that are to appear white in the final picture should be left white from the very outset.

You create light colour shades by thinning colours. Work from light colours to dark colours. You can only lighten colours by washing out with water or thinner.

3

4

5

Pink flower

The silk shines brightly through the colours and lends the flower a gossamer, spring-like appearance.

The design is painted using very light, translucent colours. This is a good, and not too difficult exercise, for painting without white.

MATERIALS
Silk: 40 × 40 cm (16 × 16 in) crêpe de Chine
Colours: steam-fixable or iron-fixable colours
Brushes: sable brushes nos 3 and 6
Outliner: spirit-based outliner or water-soluble outliner

6

7

Technique: watercolour technique and outliner technique.

The colour sketch for this design can be found on page 97. From it prepare a transfer sketch of the outlines of the flower, stem and leaves. Paint the flower, stem and leaves on to the silk using outliner. Make sure that the lines are completely closed. Allow to dry (**1**).

Before you begin painting, mix the colours for the flower: a medium and a slightly darker bluey-pink for the petals; and a warm yellow for the centre of the flower.

The flower is painted wet-on-wet. Therefore you need to dampen the flower using water. Using the no 3 sable brush and the medium pink shade apply gentle colour edges, on the damp area, along the petal outliner lines (**2**).

8

9

The flower must remain damp during the entire painting process. In the first instance, therefore, paint only half the flower, and work quickly.

Using water, drive the colours to the edges and the middle of the flower. Then fade the colour into the white area of the petal. Each time you have done this, wash out the watercolour brush before proceeding.

Do not, however, allow the other half of the flower to dry out. Make sure that the entire flower remains damp. Do not paint over the white areas of the flower (**3**).

Apply the darker bluey-pink to the middle of the flower and use a watercolour brush to force the colour towards the outliner line of the flower's calyx (**4**).

Paint the other half of the flower in the same way as you painted the first half. The surface must remain well damp so that you can paint the colours wet-on-wet (**5**).

In order to strengthen the flower's three-dimensional effect, carefully paint another gentle, light pink shade, wet-on-wet, from the flower's outer lines towards the white area of the petals. Also paint the small bud, wet-on-wet, using pink (**6**).

Paint a little yellow into the centre of the flower (**7**).

For the leaves and the stem, mix up a medium green, a blue-green and a light blue in your colour palette. Use these colours to paint the remaining parts of the plant. Here, too, you can paint wet-on wet, thus drawing the colours into each other. This generates more movement in the flower.

For the background prepare a light yellow, pink and a few gentle blue shades. Dampen the background area well and then use a no 6 sable brush to draw the colours, wet-on-wet, into one another. Make sure that you do not paint everything evenly; allow the white of the silk to shine through in a few places. Thiscreates an atmospheric background, and the picture acquires a spring-like radiance (**8**).

8 With a pastel background, the painting takes on a spring-like appearance.

9 An alternative colourway for a moodier effect.

10 The original colour sketch.

10

Creating designs

Flowers sway in the summer wind. The sunlight makes their colours shine. Deep red, warm yellow and rich green are all reminiscent of a wonderful summer's day. Many flowers come to mind. But when creating your design, think only of the most important aspects – the shapes and colours that best express your feelings.

FROM IDEA TO PICTURE

The less the better

Pictures are created in your head. This is a pearl of wisdom that one needs to remember from time to time when it comes to painting. There is no special recipe for creativity; there are, however, among the enormous variety of creative possibilities, a few useful tools from which you should select those that best suit you and then use them to the best of your ability.

Before you start, ask yourself what you are trying to achieve: would you like to produce something representative; are you looking for a balanced shape or attractive colours;

do you have a specific theme in mind; or do you want to express a particular feeling? Choose a concrete image for your design that represents your intuitive idea. The design might be a landscape, a still life, a figurative representation or a free pattern, a traditional decoration or an abstract one.

Look around you. Often you will find something close by that reflects your idea or feeling: it might be the warm brown-red of the brick wall in your garden; the shells gathered on your last holiday; some pieces of fruit on the window ledge; a photograph of a bay where you like to go for walks. No design is trivial if it is

inspired by an idea or a feeling. Reach for your pencil, charcoal or brush and sketch your picture idea. The sketch does not have to be perfect, just a first draft. Equally, do not worry about detail. The fundamental mood of the design must reflect your idea. You can always improve on it later. Perhaps you would like to develop something by simply playing with ideas. Go ahead and do it. Experiment with different shapes and colours.

It is important to use appropriate materials, even at the initial sketch stage. A pencil is good for drawing lines and shapes; a watercolour brush is more appropriate for colour compositions.

The designs on these two pages were painted in watercolours because this is a very appropriate technique for silk painting (see page 64). But silk painting is multi-faceted. You could just as easily prepare your designs using clearly defined shapes that you then paint in full (see 'Outliner Technique' on page 36).

It is advisable to reduce the designs down to the most essential features. Including all the fine detail at the very outset makes the work more difficult and distracts you from expressing yourself in an actual silk painting.

Landscape
A landscape can be designed using just a few brushstrokes. In this design the light, muted colours and the clear structure are of key significance (**1**).

Scribbles
Roughly sketched designs are called scribbles. They enable you quickly to retain designs and ideas that come to mind. Later you can develop you designs from these scribbles (**2**).

1

USING PHOTOGRAPHS

Selecting the right scene

The world is full of pictures, even in your immediate surroundings. All you have to do is find them and develop an eye for them. The flowers in the vase, at the window or in the garden, for example. Go to the zoo and take your camera with you. You will come home with many stimulating ideas.

Photography provides precisely the right training for the eye to capture good designs. As you look through the viewfinder, select a view,

1

establish the centre and structure of the picture. Many painters and graphic designers use a camera to seek out ideas. Using a camera you will quickly find a suitable shot, particularly when it comes to landscape designs.

Also, look at other people's photographs in books, newspapers and magazines. These will show you new ways of looking at things. Collect photographs that you find appealing, for example photographs of plants, insects, landscapes and surface structures. To create attractive patterns make a collection of ornaments, old tiles and art nouveau designs. You will soon have an extensive picture archive at your disposal which could be a great help to you when it comes to finding a design.

Collages

Turn the hunt for designs into a game. Bring together lots of individual details into one picture. You can also cut up your designs and mount them on card to create a collage. The results are often unexpected and can lead to highly imaginative designs.

The detail

Before taking a photograph or other draft as your initial sketch, you will have to decide which detail of it will be represented in the final picture. An adjustable frame is very useful at this point. Cut out two right angles from a piece of card; the sides should be between 20 and 30 cm (8–12 in) long. Move both the right angles across the design until you have the right detail. You will be surprised to see how many good details there are for a design. Experiment a little with the adjustable frame. Often you will come across designs and patterns that you had not noticed before.

The art of omission

Many sketches and photographs present a major disadvantage when it comes to silk painting: they contain too much detail. So if you want to use a photograph for a design you will need to simplify it considerably. To do this, place a piece of tracing paper over the picture and draw only those lines and outlines that are really important for the composition of the design. In the main this means dividing the picture into its foreground, middle ground and background, plus the rough outlines

2

of the most important objects and details. Using these lines you can envisage the later appearance your picture will have; you can also alter these lines where necessary.

Colour experiments

You can transfer the sketch to watercolour paper (see Enlargement and Reduction on page 115) and paint the design using watercolours. Painting watercolours on paper is very similar to the watercolour technique in silk painting; in other words, even at this stage of designing, you can try out many of the effects you may wish to use.

If you find painting in watercolours too complicated, create your colour designs using coloured pencils or charcoal. The colour sketches are very important. Paint several versions of the design using different colours. The mere choice of colours can have a major effect on the statement your

picture makes (see A Lesson in Colour on page 84). When creating the design, think about whether it is suitable for silk painting techniques.

Every technique has its own idiosyncrasies. Some effects, such as hatching, are very difficult to achieve in silk painting; others, such as colour runs, work very well.

Pines in the snow

This photograph exudes an unreal, almost suspended, mood. It is an attractive and stimulating starting point for a watercolour silk painting design (**1**).

The initial colour design

The first step is to transfer the most important outlines from the photograph; the design is then painted using watercolours (**2**).

Designing using a mixture of techniques

Coloured pencils are very good for drawing colour sketches. To the left

of picture 3 you can see the fine-tipped coloured pencils made by Schwan-Stabilo. These can be used to draw both clear, well-delimited lines as well as to hatch and cover large areas. You can use them with water. They can be used to achieve delicate colour shades.

On the right of the picture you can see coloured drawing charcoal (made by Carb-Othello), which here take the form of coloured pencils. These pencils can be used in many different ways. The colours are rich and intense. They can be smudged to create very delicate colour runs. The colour application is opaque. Therefore you can also work on coloured and dark backgrounds. The pencils are particularly suitable for colouring both large areas and very fine lines. They too can be used with water. However, the colours are neither fast when handling nor smudge proof. Therefore, after painting they must be protected using a fixing spray.

Almost all the colour sketches in this book were made using Carb-Othello and Schwan-Stabilo fine-tipped colour pencils. These two types of pencil can easily be used together or combined with watercolours.

The upper part of the picture was painted using watercolours. You can use your silk painting brushes to do this.

Lead pencils, like the one shown in the centre right of the picture, are indispensable for drawing scribbles and sketches. Use hard pencils (7H) to draw light, fine lines, and very soft pencils (8B) to draw dark and thick lines. For sketching, HB and B pencils will suffice.

The picture shows only a small selection of the available variety of good sketching equipment.

A CORNER DESIGN – BINDWEED

The Bindweed is an attractive design which is perfect for use as a corner motif. You can further develop the tendrils and leaves so that they create a frame around an area.

When working this design try to ensure that it is not only the plant's shape that has a natural appearance but also the outlines of the black area. These so-called 'negative' shapes should also have their own inner harmony.

Transfer sketch
The clear, decorative flow of the lines is very well suited to the outliner technique. Remember, even at the drafting stage, to make sure that all the shapes are closed. You can then paint these easily later (**1**).

Colour sketch
The sketch is made in colour using charcoal pencils. The colours can be massaged using cotton wool buds. In this way you can create very gentle colour transitions. This allows you to assess the effect of the wet-on-wet technique at the design stage. Draw the flower in both strong and soft colours and then decide on your own preferred colour combination. Another colour suggestion can be seen on page 106 (**2**, **3** and **4**).

Bindweed
On the black background the gentle colours of the bindweed acquire a strong brilliance. The light petals seem to suggest that the flower is sucking the light into its calyx.

Transfer the sketch on to silk and draw the lines using spirit-based outliner. Allow the picture to dry. Before you start to paint, mix up the following colours: a light blue shade for the leaves and a darker, red-violet shade for the delicate contours on the outer edge of the petals and for the centre of the flower; also mix a pale red-violet for the bud. For the leaves, stem and tendrils, mix up various green shades using emerald green and may green; warm these shades using a little sky blue to make a blue-green; lemon to make a warm, yellowy green; and ruby red to make an olive green.

Apply light and medium tones of the mixtures made. Now you can paint the flower, wet-on-wet, in the appropriate colours. So that the flower appears three-dimensional, leave a little white showing; do the same with the bud. Apply the red-violet colour shade to the centre of the flower and, using the tip of the brush and a very small amount of colour, carefully paint the red-violet contour to the outer edge of the flower's petals. Leave the flower to dry.

1 and 2

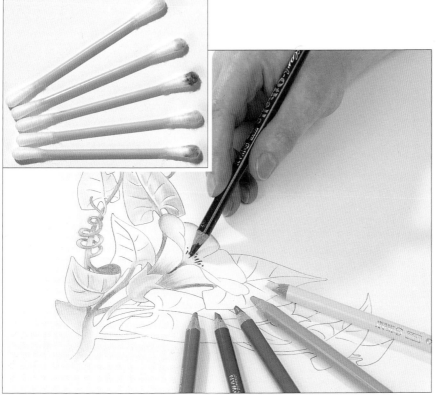

3 and 4

Materials
Silk: 40×40 cm (16×16 in) crêpe de Chine
Colours: steam-fixable colours
Top row of colour chart: black, emerald, ruby red, sky blue
Bottom row of colour chart: may green, lemon, violet
Brushes: no 7 sable brush and a watercolour brush
Outliner: spirit-based outliner
Technique: outliner technique and wet-on-wet technique

Take a dry brush and, in small, rapid brushstrokes and dabs, paint the stamen in a slightly darker red-violet colour shade over the red-violet colour that has already been applied. Paint the tendrils and the leaf structure, wet-on-wet, using the various green shades; this will give life to the plant.

Finally, paint the background an even black. Work carefully around the delicate tendrils and make sure that no colour runs under the outliner lines. Leave the entire picture to dry, then fix and clean it. On the black background even the gentle shades of green, blue and pink will have a strong brilliance. You should take this effect into account when choosing the colours for your picture. Often you will not need to use strong colours if your design is to have a black background (**5**).

5

DECORATION

Fashion and home designs

On these pages you can see some designs for scarves, shawls and cushions. You should use them as inspiration for your own personal fashion and home designs. Silk painting is particularly suitable for dresses, kimonos, blouses, skirts, small bags, collars and cuffs and the like, as well as for curtains, lampshades or covers.

Designs for shawls, scarves and cushions

When you are making a design, think about the eventual format it will take. In the case of scarves and cushions, the basic surface shape is usually 'a rectangle or a square. Scarves, however, are usually folded diagonally so that when they are worn the shape seen is in fact a triangle. The design should therefore be based on a triangle shape. The design should not only fit the shape, it also needs to be positioned appropriately on the silk.

The Bindweed design (**1**) is triangular and suitably positioned on the silk for a scarf. The shape can be folded diagonally without the design being lost.

The lily design (**2**), on the other hand, is designed for a cushion cover. This design cannot be folded, unless of course you position the flower in a corner and rearrange the leaves. The designs in pictures 3 and 4 have an even spread of colour over the surface area used. No significant detail that would always need to be visible has been employed. These designs are therefore effective whether seen in their entirety or when the silk is folded.

When designing a scarf yet another practical note to take into account is that the opposite corners of the scarf will become intertwined. The colours in opposite corners must therefore match. This is a point that you need to consider when making the very first draft of your design.

1

2

3

Tip: Cut out your colour sketch in paper and fold it as if it were a scarf. This will show you if the corners of the scarf actually match.

If you create your design as a mirror image or symmetrically, this usually makes it very easy to fold and the effect is an harmonious one.

Equally, rows in a design, particularly in decorative silk painting, have a very attractive effect. This is especially the case with patterns, flowers and tendrils which are very effective as borders and repeated themes.

When creating a design you should make sure that where motifs actually touch one another, they go to-gether. Individual motifs, such as the flowers in pictures 1 and 2, are held together by a painted border. This means they are not lost on a scarf or shawl.

A painted border has the same effect as a picture frame; it draws the picture out of its surroundings and at the same time gives it a clear boundary. Of course, all designs can be painted without a border.

Borders also create a very good effect on larger cushion covers (90 × 90 cm, 36 × 36 in). Smaller cushions (40 × 40 cm, 16 × 16 in) are usually better without a border, however, as this makes the internal design too small.

Bindweed
An attractive corner motif for scarfs and shawls that works very well, even when folded diagonally (**1**).

Flower
This design makes full use of the cushion format. The main focus is the flower, positioned in the centre of the design. The broad border holds the design together visually. Some variations can be seen on page 138 (**2**).

Coloured Leaves
This design was made after a walk through woods and fields in bloom. It can be used as either a full-format or a folded design. Variations of it can be seen in the section 'Design Ideas' beginning on page 116 (**3**).

Stars and Leaves
This design has a wide edge and a scatter pattern around the main central motif. The black background makes the gentle colours bolder and binds the many small shapes. This is a decorative design for the home and for fashion accessories. A variation of the design can be seen on page 124 (**4**).

4

COLLAGES

Dream Tree from the East

Nature often provides examples, inspiration and ideas. The concept of the Dream Tree came from pressed leaves; this is a leaf collage.

It is very simple. You press the leaves between two thick layers of paper (absorbent paper, paper napkins or blotting paper) weighted down with books. Make sure that the leaves lie next to and not on top of one another. It will be about ten days before the leaves are ready.

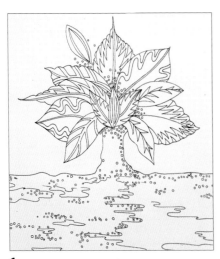

1

The pressed leaves can easily be made into a collage. Move them around until you are happy with the arrangement. For the tree design it is advisable to organise them in as natural a way as possible.

When you are happy with the collage, fix the leaves to the paper using multi-purpose glue.

To transfer the design, lay a piece of tracing paper over the collage and, using a soft pencil, trace the shapes. You will use this basic design to develop your silk painting (**1**).

In this picture you see a collage made up of various pressed leaves glued to wrapping paper decorated with stars (**2**).

MATERIALS
Silk: 42 × 42 cm (16½ × 16½ in) crêpe de Chine
Colours: iron-fixable silk painting colours
Top row of colour chart: blue, olive green, black, chestnut brown
Middle row of colour chart: turquoise, violet
Bottom row of colour chart: yellow, aubergine, pink, claret

Brushes: no 8 sable brush and a watercolour brush
Outliner: colourless spirit-based outliner
Technique: overlaying technique and watercolour technique (wet-on-wet)

At this stage of the procedure the design looks as if it has been gently blown into position. Mix a light turquoise and a light yellow in your colour palette. Dampen the silk thoroughly using water. Then quickly apply first the turquoise and then the yellow using diagonal brushstrokes. Force out the colour using a watercolour brush. Allow the picture to dry (**4**).

Draw the design using colourless spirit-based outliner and mask the initial dots. Paint the details on the leaves using the appropriate colours. Mix a turquoise green using turquoise and a little yellow. Paint the inner parts of the leaves, wet-on-wet, using colours that flow into one another. Slightly darken the two background shades, turquoise and yellow, and mix a claret red and a violet to the same depth. Use these colour shades to paint a second layer of colour over the background so that the corresponding colours lie over one another. Paint the trunk brown, wet-on-wet. Also using the wet-on-wet technique, paint the ground in dark and light yellow and in brown shades. Allow the painting to dry.

Using spirit-based outliner, mask

2

3

lots of dots on the background. Allow these to dry. Make up a light grey in a jar using a lot of water and some black and then test the colour shade on a small piece of silk. Apply water to the background, making sure that no pools of water form. Apply the grey shade to the damp silk using rapid diagonal brush-strokes across the background. Do not, however, cover the entire background! This will give it far more vitality. Work quickly so that no hard edges form (**5**).

4

Dream Tree by Night
The tree is drawn initially using colourless gutta; then it is painted. The effects on the foreground are created using salt. This variation on the design, using different colours, is also very attractive. Take inspiration from your collection of leaves (**3**).

5

Leaf collage

Experiment with colours, patterns and shapes. Occasionally put things together that do not seem to go together. Collages are always good for producing surprises. Take your inspiration from printed wrapping paper, carpets, old ornaments and crazy graffiti. By way of contrast to these, select a well structured leaf. The very life of a collage stems from the contrast between graphic structures and natural shapes. Have fun as you experiment!

Transfer sketch

The centrepiece here is a twig with its leaves. The effect is emphasised by the lines of the individual planes that stretch from the twig towards the edge of the design. The background is highly structured, contrasting with the solid colour blocks of the leaves. The result is that the leaves are clearly distinguishable from the background (**1**).

Leaf collage on a chalk background

Pastel chalks are used to apply a pattern on to dyed Ingres paper which is then fixed. A pressed twig with leaves is then stuck on to the paper.

The transfer sketch is made on the basis of this collage. Various small patterns form between the graphic lines (**2**).

Leaf collage

This is a cheerful design and you can use it to experiment with colours, patterns and textures (**4**).

MATERIALS
Silk: 30 × 40 cm (12 × 16 in) crêpe de Chine
Colours: iron-fixable silk painting colours
Top row of colour chart: yellow, pink
Second row of colour chart: aubergine, violet
Third row of colour chart: turquoise, turquoise green
Bottom row of colour chart: deep green, silver grey
Brush: no 8 sable
Outliner: black outliner (either water-soluble or spirit-based)
Technique: outliner technique, wet-on-wet technique and wash-out technique
Transfer the design to silk and draw the outlines using black outliner. Leave this to dry.

Paint the leaf, wet-on-wet, in turquoise green and turquoise. Apply the relevant colours to the background. Do not paint beyond the

outliner lines into neighbouring fields. Let the colours flow into one another, wet-on-wet, under the ring pattern. Some of the dot pattern shapes can be painted on to damp colour areas and some on to dry colour. A few dots can also be washed out. You do not have to keep to the colours and shapes shown here. Be creative and let your imagination run free. For example, you might also apply some salt effects or single shades to some of the background areas.

1 The transfer sketch for your design.

2 This is how you apply the collage.

3 Colour chart.

4 The finished leaf collage – imaginatively created using colours and patterns.

1

2

3

ATMOSPHERIC PERSPECTIVES

Early-morning Landscape

Slowly the dawn breaks. The sky turns a yellowy red and pink before the sun comes up over the horizon. The landscape is still enveloped in the blue light of night. In the valleys the mist is lifting. The eye is drawn across them and into the distance beyond.

This picture has enormous depth. The effect is created by the colours becoming increasingly paler and lighter the further up the picture they go, while the dark, strong colours at the base of the picture force their way into the foreground. We know about this effect – known as atmospheric perspectives – from the 'Lesson in Colour' (beginning on page 84).

MATERIALS
Silk: 40 × 30 cm (16 × 12 in) crêpe de Chine
Colours: steam-fixable silk painting colours

Top row of colour chart: violet, rhodamine
Bottom row of colour chart: sky blue, lemon
Brushes: no 8 sable brush, watercolour brush
Outliner: spirit-based outliner
Technique: outliner technique and watercolour technique (wet-on-wet)

Transfer drawing
Enlarge the transfer drawing to the format of your choice (see page 115) (**1**).

Colour sketch
Charcoal pencils (Carb-Othello) are good for creating delicate colour moods. They are opaque and can be smudged into one another, thus enabling you to create atmospheric perspective, even at the colour sketch stage.

A layer of dark, opaque colours is applied to the foreground. The further up the picture you proceed, the thinner the layer of colour and the lighter the colours become (**2**).

Early-morning Landscape
Copy the lines from the initial drawing using spirit-based outliner. Allow this to dry.

For the sky mix in your colour palette a light and a dark yellow, a light blue thinned considerably with water, and a light pink. Paint the sky in these shades using the wet-on-wet technique.

For the mountains mix several violet shades, a light blue shade and a pink-violet. Start with the dark colours in the foreground and then the further back the mountains are meant to appear, the lighter the colour should become. In this picture the colours are not as contrasting as those in the colour sketch. This enhances the atmospheric effect. It is further strengthened by the fact that, after the second chain of mountains, the colours fade into the white of the silk the nearer to the outliner line they get. The effect is

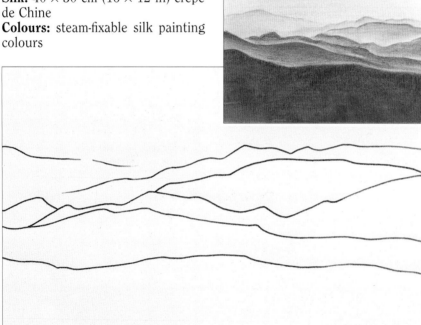

1 and 2

3

that the mountains appear to be emerging from the mist.

In a few places the outliner lines are no longer visible.

This is not a particularly easy technique. Using a watercolour brush, work from below towards the colour that you are drawing into the picture from above. This forces the col-our into the upper part of the mountain chain. Fade the colour down into the silk, thus achieving gentle transitions. Allow the painting to dry, then fix it and finally clean it (**4**).

This landscape reminds us of the soft light of early morning. This effect is created through the careful use of contrasts: the clear contours of the mountains gently fade down-wards with the result that the mountain ridges appear to be floating above the mist. The blue-violet col-ours of the land stand out well against the yellow-violet of the sky, and this in turn rises bright and light above the heavy, dark mountains.

4

Mountains in the Morning Light

In this variation of the picture on page 113, the colour nuances are applied in far more striking contrasts, although the shades are not as strongly graduated as in the colour sketch.

Furthermore, the colours are not as watery as in the last picture. No white spaces have been left. Thus, the outliner lines remain clearly visible. As a result, the picture's effect is more striking, although it has less depth than the colour sketch and picture 4. The mountains, clearly delineated silhouettes, stand out from one another. The effect is more a result of their soft, flowing shapes than of the perspective. The picture thus acquires an air of unreality which is further emphasised by the contrast between very hard and soft colours.

5

ENLARGEMENT AND REDUCTION

In order to enlarge or reduce a design, lay a piece of tracing paper across the design and draw the most important lines. Then draw a grid of vertical and horizontal lines across the drawing. Draw the same grid on to a separate sheet of paper, but this time increase or decrease the distance between the lines depending on whether you wish to enlarge or reduce the design. It is not too difficult to draw the outlines on to the second grid so that the lines intersect at the same points on the second grid as they do on the first. In the pictures on these two pages you can see how the landscape can be enlarged or reduced.

Of course, it is easier to enlarge or reduce the initial sketch using a photocopier. If necessary, you can copy various sections of the picture and then later reconstitute the whole. Before you make any copies, go over the most important lines using a felt pen so that they are clearly visible on the copies you make.

You can also make a slide of the initial design and then project it directly on to a piece of silk that has been stretched across a frame. If you are using a projector, you can enlarge or reduce the motif by altering the distance between the silk and the projector or by adjusting the zoom lens accordingly.

If you have an episcope or an overhead projector at your disposal you can project the initial design directly on to the white silk. An 'Artograph', available from graphic arts suppliers, will fulfil the same function.

Trace the projected outlines on to the silk using a soft pencil.

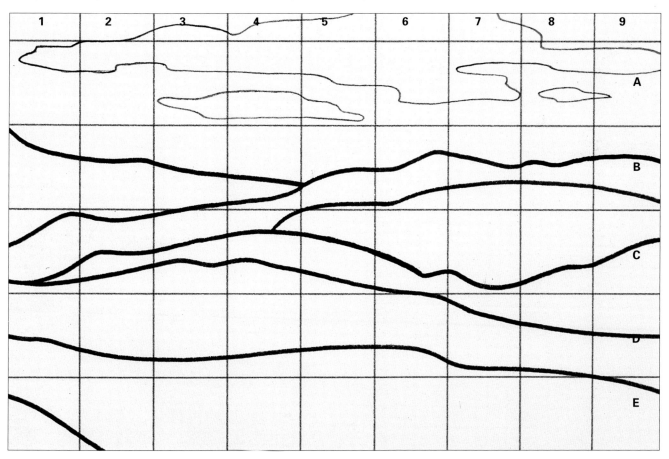

Design ideas

Be it clear, graphic styling or poetically flowing streams of colour, every creative element has its own inimitable effect which arouses very specific sensations and feelings. How you awake these different emotions is up to you. Using the techniques of silk painting you can create the pictures of your dreams.

SCATTERED LEAVES

Scattered leaves – they lie where they have fallen until another gust of wind swirls them on.

This is a game with natural shapes and decorative detail which you can vary to your heart's delight, as shown in the pictures on this and the previous pages.

Painting can be composed using the same shapes and patterns yet achieve completely different effects. The picture on the right appears soft and dainty; the leaves on the black background on the previous pages appear vivid and almost explosive. The black makes the colours glow. This effect is further strengthened by the contrast in the colours chosen, namely warm yellow and red shades set against a cool blue. The leaves on the black background are clearly structured. Their shapes, through mosaic-like details, dissolve into the black surface. The picture in its entirety creates a highly contrasting, colourful, graphic effect.

You can see a variation of this design on page 107 in Coloured Leaves. The picture on the right, however, has a far lighter and softer effect. The leaf shapes are more realistic and the colours are gentler, with each graduated colour matched against the next. This design was created from a leaf collage.

Materials

Silk: 60 × 60 cm (24 × 24 in) crêpe de Chine

Colours: iron-fixable silk painting colours

Top row of colour chart: yellow, pink

Second row of colour chart: claret, violet

Third row of colour chart: turquoise, turquoise green

Bottom row of colour chart: deep green, olive green

Brushes: no 9 sable brush

Outliner: black outliner (either water-soluble or spirit-based)

Technique: outliner technique and watercolour technique

Scattered Leaves

The picture on pages 116–17 was painted using colourless outliner without wet-on-wet runs.

Picture 3 on the right, however, was created using black outliner. Allow this to dry. Stir the outliner well

1

2

before you begin. Paint a test on paper to see whether it flows well. Mix light, medium and full tones using the colours listed above and paint the surfaces as in the picture. The leaves and decoration are painted partly using the wet-on-wet technique and partly on to dry silk. You can read about the differences between painting on wet and dry silk on page 68. Allow the painting to dry and then fix it.

3

COLOURED OUTLINERS

Dots, stripes and stars

You can create unusual effects using simple shapes such as dots, stripes, wavy lines and stars. Coloured outliners give designs highlights. Many of these outliners have a metallic finish. They are opaque and shimmer in various colours.

For the purpose of comparison, the pictures were also painted using colourless outliners. These have a more transparent and lighter effect.

Painting with coloured outliner

Coloured outliners must be well stirred before they are applied to the silk; this ensures even distribution of the colour particles. After stirring, leave the outliner to stand for a short time. Then paint a test on to a piece of paper to see if the liquid flows evenly. Now you can begin to paint on the silk. Coloured outliners must dry thoroughly after application.

Using the coloured outliners produced by some manufacturers you can not only draw strong lines but also colour open areas. Follow the manufacturer's instructions precisely and test how the coloured out-

liners can be worked and how they react. This is particularly applicable if you are creating paintings for fashion or home articles. Some products form a slightly sticky surface; others change as a result of washing or cleaning.

MATERIALS
Silk: 21 × 19 cm (8½ × 8 in) habutai silk
Colours: iron-fixable silk painting colours
Colour chart for stars and stripes
Top row: yellow, azure, claret, aubergine
Bottom row: turquoise, turquoise green, violet, black
Colour chart for dots and stripes
Top row: yellow, aubergine, claret, violet, black
Bottom row: pink, turquoise green, smoke blue, turquoise
Brushes: no 8 sable brush and a watercolour brush
Outliner: coloured (pictures 5 and 8) and colourless (pictures 6 and 7) outliners
Technique: outliner technique and watercolour technique

The method of painting is very similar for all the pictures. The Stars and Stripes motif in pictures 5 and 6 is

carried out using the outliner and watercolour (wet-on-wet) techniques. For the Dots and Stripes design – pictures 7 and 8 – you need use only the outliner technique.

To create the Stars and Stripes design, using colourless or coloured outliner draw the lines as in the transfer sketch in picture 1. Leave to dry. Paint the patterns and stars in the appropriate colours. Then apply water to every other stripe and paint, wet-on-wet, a flow into the stripes using diluted azure, turquoise and turquoise green.

Paint the other stripes black. Leave to dry and then fix.

1 Transfer sketch for stars and stripes.

2 Transfer sketch for dots and stripes.

3 Colour sketches.

4 Colour chart for picture 5, stars and stripes, using colourless outliner.

5 Stars and stripes, painted using coloured outliner.

6 Stars and stripes using colourless outliner.

7 Dots and stripes using colourless outliner.

8 Dots and stripes using coloured outliner.

9 Colour chart for picture 7, dots and stripes.

1

2

3

4

5

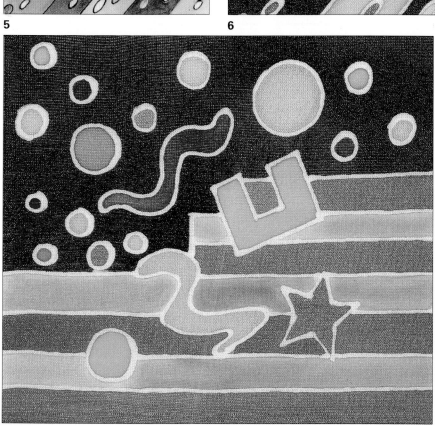

6

7

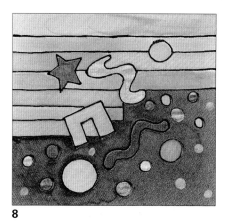

8

9

YELLOW SUN AND YELLOW FLASH

Coloured outliners strengthen the structure of a painting. The black lines emphasise the shapes of the areas of colour. Dots of outliner give the surface vitality. The outliners shimmer gold, silver and pink. Embossed structures have a metallic shine, depending on the play of light (**1**).

If painted using colourless outliner the individual shapes appear to recede. The effect of the overall picture is a gentle one (**5**).

Yellow sun

MATERIALS
Silk: 21 × 19cm (8½ × 8in) habutai silk
Colours: iron-fixable silk painting colours
Top row of colour chart: yellow, heather
Second row of colour chart: aubergine, turquoise green
Third row of colour chart: pink, turquoise
Bottom row of colour chart: azure, black
Brushes: no 8 sable brush and a watercolour brush
Outliner: coloured and colourless outliner

Technique: outliner technique and watercolour technique

Transfer the lines from the transfer drawing on to the silk. Draw the lines using either coloured or colourless outliner, depending on how strongly structured you wish to make your picture. Leave the painting to dry thoroughly. Now paint the small areas in the appropriate colours (**3**).

Now, using the wet-on-wet technique, paint the background using azure, turquoise and turquoise green. Leave to dry and then fix (**5**).

The colour chart for picture 8, Yellow Flash, was painted using coloured outliner (**6**).

2

3   **4**

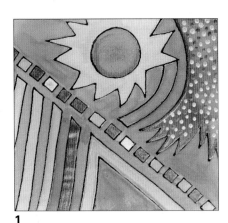

1

5

6

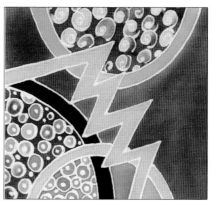

7

Colour sketches for Yellow Sun and Yellow flash (**7**).

The coloured outliner lines in picture 8 emphasise its various levels. The individual shapes appear to be lying one on top of the other; the structure is more clear-cut (**8**).

The gentle effects of silk painting can be better seen if the picture is painted using colourless outliner. The effect of the design is now far more friendly (**9**).

Yellow flash

MATERIALS
Silk: 21 × 19 cm (8½ × 8 in) habutai silk

Colours: iron-fixable silk painting colours
Top row of colour chart: yellow, pink
Middle row of colour chart: aubergine, turquoise
Bottom row of colour chart: turquoise green, black
Brushes: no 8 sable brush and a watercolour brush
Outliner: coloured and colourless outliner
Technique: outliner technique and watercolour technique

Draw the outlines using coloured or colourless outliner. Leave to dry. Paint all the surfaces, except for the area inside the turquoise-green ring, in the given colours.

Using the wet-on-wet technique, paint the area inside the turquoise-green ring. Paint the yellow sections first, then apply aubergine to the yellow squiggles. From inside the squiggles, use the watercolour brush to work against the squiggles so that soft runs are created. Leave to dry and then fix.

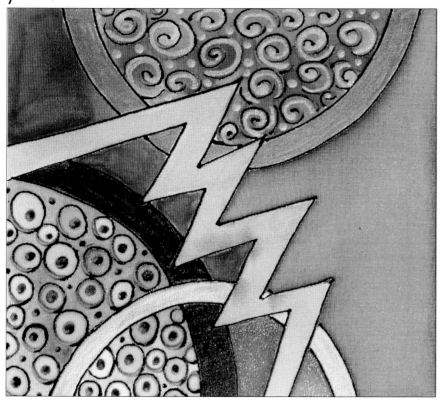

8

9

SHAPES AND COLOURS

Stars and Leaves

Stars, leaves, triangles, circles and other geometric shapes can be distributed playfully across the silk as if they had been scattered over it.

Many small elements, such as dots for example, can be used to form larger shapes. This prevents the pattern from falling apart. The two versions (pictures 4 and 5) may well have very different effects but only in as much as different colours and different silk painting techniques have been used.

Picture 4 was painted using the wet-on-wet and the outliner technique. In this version the black outliner lines hold together the small individual parts.

Picture 5 combines the wet-on-wet technique with the overlaying technique. This makes possible spirit-based outlines reserved with colour runs. In this picture the colour effects have been reversed: the background is one single colour and the shapes have many iridescent colours. The shapes and colours of the details are particularly effective set against a black background.

Perhaps you actually recognise the pattern? It can be seen on page 107 in picture 4 as a broad, patterned border. Both the arrangement of the shapes and the colours in this scatter pattern can easily be varied.

MATERIALS

Silk: 33 × 27 cm (13 × 10½ in) habutai silk
Colours: iron-fixable silk painting colours
Top row of colour chart: yellow, claret, blue, turquoise green, black
Bottom row of colour chart: pink, violet, turquoise, orange
Brushes: no 8 sable brush and a watercolour brush
Outliner: black outliner
Technique: outliner technique and watercolour technique

Stars and Leaves (4)

Draw the outlines using black outliner. Leave to dry thoroughly. All black areas should be painted using black silk paint and not black outliner. Paint the small patterns in the given colours. The background colours are placed next to one another on the dry silk and then drawn into the adjacent areas, which are still damp, using a watercolour brush. Try out this procedure on a small piece of silk. The background is not easy to paint. It is very important that you make a colour sketch before you begin the actual painting; the sketch should clearly show the colour distribution. This makes painting considerably easier because you have to complete the background quickly.

The silk painting does not necessarily have to incorporate all the details shown in the colour sketch. It should, however, follow the colour distribution laid down in the sketch. Leave to dry and fix.

Stars and Leaves (5)

This silk painting was carried out using spirit-based outliner and steam-fixable silk painting colours. However, you may also paint it using spirit-based outliner and iron-fixable silk painting colours. As the latter is rather complicated and time-consuming, it is probably easier to stick to the method used here. The important thing about this picture is

1

2

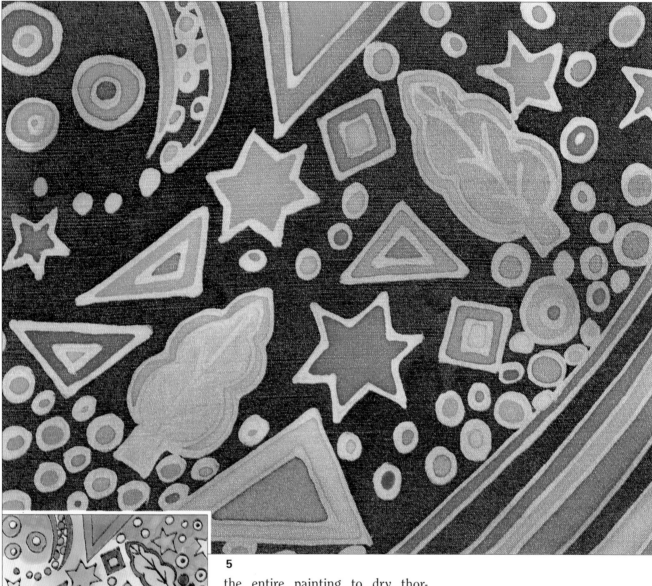

5

the entire painting to dry thoroughly. Paint the inner areas of the pattern using strong colours. These colours will to some extent mix with the colours already there in the background. Read more about this in the section entitled 'The World of Colours' (on page 84).

If you wish to exclude the possibility of unexpected mix effects arising, paint tone-on-tone over the background colours.

Apply the background around the pattern, using black. Finally, steam-fix your silk painting and clean it.

4

the colour-reserved outliner lines. Apply the background using the wet-on-wet technique and light colour shades, then leave to dry. Draw the pattern over this using colourless spirit-based outliner. Then leave

1 Transfer sketch.

2 Colour sketch.

3 Colour chart.

4 Stars and Leaves painted using black outliner. The black lines emphasise the individual shapes of the pattern.

5 Stars and Leaves painted using colour-reserved spirit-based outliner lines. The black background links the shapes and allows the colours to shine. The colour runs in the outliner-reserved areas lend this silk painting an air of mystery.

TRIANGULAR BIRD

This small bird lives in a geometrical world. And yet despite the severity of the lines, the effect is still an amusing one. The colours are clear. The pastel nature of the shades lends the picture a brightness that reflects the spirit of the little bird. The bird blends into the colours of its surroundings. Thus the picture creates an harmonious feel, in spite of its graphic precision.

The only difference between pictures 4 and 5 is the colours used. The blue of picture 4 reflects a night-time mood. It was painted using colourless spirit-based outliner. The outlines, which appear white, contrast attractively with the dark blue and violet tones of the background. Black outlines would not have a contrasting effect if set against colours very similar to black, and thus the bird would be barely distinguishable.

The bright, colourful picture 5 is quite different. Its light colours are reminiscent of spring. Here the black outlines are particularly effective. The clear character of the picture is a result of the base colours red, yellow and blue, which have been considerably diluted, in the background. Thanks to the use of bright colours, the bird in this picture appears much more cheerful.

If you want to vary the colours, make sure that the bird always stands out clearly from the background by using contrasting outlines or colours.

MATERIALS
Silk: 28 × 34 cm (11 × 13½ in) habutai silk
Colours: iron-fixable silk painting colours
Top row of colour chart: yellow, claret
Middle row of colour chart: violet, blue
Bottom row of colour chart: turquoise, turquoise green
Brush: no 8 sable brush
Outliner: black outliner
Hair dryer
Technique: outliner technique and watercolour technique (wet-on-wet)

Triangular Bird in Spring
Draw the outlines using black outliner, leave these to dry thoroughly and then paint the design in the given colours. Using water, thin the colours to light, pastel shades. Apply the colours to the dry silk and then, in places, paint these into one another using a watercolour brush. Leave the small patterns white.

When painting the beak, use a hair dryer so that the red does not run too far. Leave the painting to dry and then fix in the normal way (**5**).

Triangular Bird at Night
This design was painted using spirit-based outliner and steam-fixable silk painting colours.

Paint the design on to white silk using colourless spirit-based outliner; do not paint the small patterns! Apply a very light blue-green colour shade to the area with the dot pattern and a very light violet shade to the area containing the triangles and squares pattern. Allow the silk to dry.

Next, paint the bird and the remaining areas using the given colours. Paint the dots and the triangles and squares using spirit-based outliner. Leave to dry. Over this, using the wet-on-wet technique, paint the dotted area blue-green and violet shades, and the area with the triangles and squares pattern blue-green shades. Leave to dry, fix and clean (**4**).

Tip: You could also use salt to create a different effect in the patterned area, or you could wash out patterns from the area.

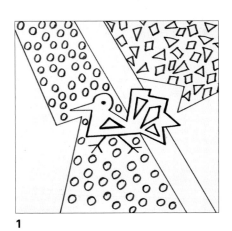

1

2

3

1 The very graphic structure of the picture is clearly shown on the transfer sketch. At the painting stage, however, the colours soften this effect.

2 Colour chart.

3 The colour sketch clearly shows the picture's spring-like and clear character.

4 The trick with the Triangular Bird at Night is the colour-reserved, spirit-based outliner dots and triangular and square shapes. They inject life into this otherwise very linear picture.

5 The Triangular Bird in spring picks up the colours of the background, albeit the opposite way round. This is yet another way of adding excitement to the picture.

4 and 5

WITHOUT WHITE

At Sea

Blue, green and white are the colours of the sea. No other colours are used for this picture. They express distance and a feeling of solitude because the colours of nearness and warmth, ie the red-yellow shades, are absent.

This effect is further reinforced by the gentle, wet-on-wet colour runs which, in places, are spread very softly into the white silk. In other words, the white of the silk is incorporated into the composition of the picture because the colour white is not available in silk painting (see World of Colours beginning on page 84).

With the exception of the dark–light contrast, contrasts are absent from this picture. Thus, no one element dominates particularly. The impression given is one of a peaceful, natural state. You could experiment by painting the boat in yellow or red shades. This will break the peaceful mood of the landscape and will look like an alien element. The boat fits better with the overall mood of the picture if you use just a few lines to give it an air of solitude and calm.

Colour sketch

From this picture you can clearly see how important it is to make a colour sketch before you start to paint. Many white areas are included in the colour composition and these must be left white from the very outset. As there are many colour flows in this picture it is a good idea to base the silk painting on the colour sketch (**2**).

At Sea

A solitary boat rests on the shore; it is taking a short break from its sea crossing. Parallel horizontal lines and restrained shades of blue-green to white emphasise the impression of calm and distance (**4**).

MATERIALS
Silk: 40 × 60 cm (16 × 24 in) crêpe de Chine
Colours: steam-fixable silk painting colours
Top row of colour chart: azure, emerald
Bottom row of colour chart: brilliant blue
Brushes: sable brushes nos 8 and 3 and a watercolour brush
Outliner: colourless spirit-based outliner
Hair dryer
Technique: outliner technique and watercolour technique

Paint the design on to the silk using colourless spirit-based outliner; do not paint the grasses and the shadow lines in the upper part of the chain of hills. You will need only three colours for this picture. Before you begin painting, mix each of the following in your colour palette: light, medium and dark colour shades. Use blue colour tones for

1

2

3

the sky, the chain of hills and the boat; use blue-green shades for the water and the grasses. Dampen the silk with water.

For the sky, draw a colour run in blue tones starting at the top and working downwards. Leave a white strip across the chain of hills. This colour run must be spread very softly. As the white outliner lines of the chain of hills are intended to remain visible, draw a very light blue tone upwards along the outliner line and blend it into the white of the silk. For this, use just a tiny amount of colour in order to retain the atmosphere of the picture. Apply two different medium-blue shades to the upper hills, left and right, and allow the colour to dry a little. The silk should not dry out completely, however. Paint the darker shaded side of the hills and fix the colours using the hair dryer. This requires a little practice. An easier solution would be to prime the hills after the first application of colour (see section beginning on page 76) and then to paint the shaded side of the hills on to the primer.

Test to see if the lower part of the picture is still damp. If not, dampen the silk again using water before you continue painting. Using the wet-on-wet technique, paint the surface of the water along the outliner line in various strong blue-green shades and allow the colour to run down into the white part of the silk. Wait a moment before continuing to paint, thus allowing the colours to flow. Now paint blue-geen shades, starting from the bottom edge of the picture; allow these shades to run upwards into the white of the silk. Paint gentle colour flows, in blue-green shades, in the middle part of the picture.

Using the tip of the brush, apply darker blue-green shades to the outliner lines of the waves and underneath the boat. Before continuing to paint, allow the silk to dry.

Use a dry brush to draw the grasses in blue-green, working upwards, and then paint the sailing boat and the mast using two different shades of blue. Leave to dry, then fix and clean.

LIGHT AND SHADE

Shells on the Beach

Shells look so fragile on the beach, washed up by the tide. Mother-of-pearl shimmers like silk in gentle pink and purple. This design, with its delicate reflections and shading, is tailor-made for silk painting. The sheen of the silk emphasises the shine of mother-of-pearl. The shells look almost as if you could touch them. This effect is created using clever light and dark gradations of colour, reproducing light where it falls, and incorporating shadows beneath the shells. However, you need to bear in mind the direction of the light. In this picture, the sun is assumed to be half-way up on the left-hand side, which means that the light colour shades must face that way and the darker shading must face the opposite direction.

MATERIALS
Silk: 30 × 40 cm (12 × 16 in) habutai silk
Colours: iron-fixable silk painting colours
Top row of colour chart: yellow, pink

Second row of colour chart: lavender, violet
Third row of colour chart: claret, black
Bottom row of colour chart: dark brown
Brushes: sable brushes nos 8 and 3 and a watercolour brush
Outliner: spirit-based outliner or water-soluble outliner
Technique: outliner technique and watercolour technique

Copy the lines from the initial drawing (1 and 2), using either spirit-based outliner or water-soluble outliner. Iron-fixable colours can be fixed using steam; this is essential for the spirit-based outliner technique. You can, of course, use any appropriate steam-fixable colours. Before you begin to paint, mix various yellow, violet, pink and pale blue-pink shades in your colour palette making light, medium and dark colour gradations of each.

Paint each of the shells, working from the top left to the bottom right. All the shells are painted in the same way. Paint the scallop shell on

the bottom right of the picture as follows: dampen the shell area with water and paint in a light pink. Leave some bright white areas. Take a watercolour brush and work against the inflowing colour.

Make sure that the colours at the transition points are always well blended. The brushstrokes should always reflect the shape of the shell. Apply the first shading using a slightly darker violet-pink and use it to indicate the shape of the shell. These colours, too, should be blended using a watercolour brush. Leave the silk to dry slightly, but it should not dry out completely. Then apply further shading to the shell using medium and darker colour shades. Here you should work with a brush that is not too wet and use only a little colour. Once you have painted all the shells, use the wet-on-wet technique to fill in the background with various yellow shades and allow the silk to dry a little. Take a dry no 3 sable brush and apply the shadows under the shells and paint the dots on the sand brown. Finally, steam-fix the painting and clean (**4**).

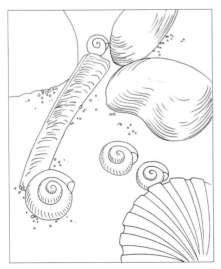

1

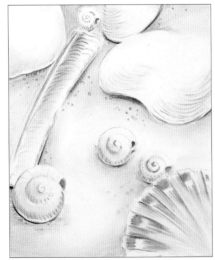

2

3

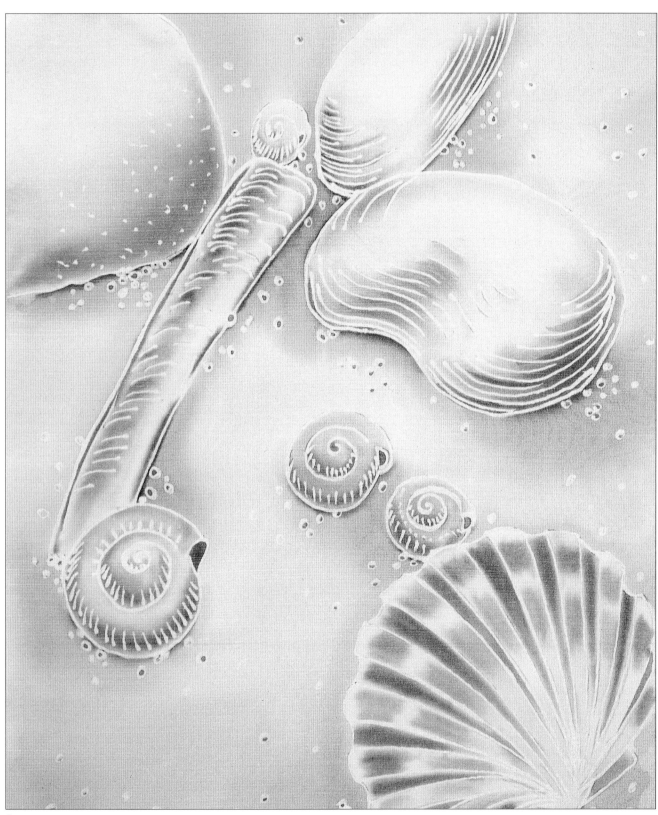

FABRIC DESIGN

Crazy Patterns

Crazy patterns are well suited to being painted on silk. Silk painting colours offer you strong means of expression ranging from intense brilliance to soft secondary colours or wonderfully light pastel shades. This broad range offers you a great many artistic possibilities. You can therefore create your colour designs and patterns according to your imagination or the sources of inspiration that surround you. This is very important for the fields in which silk painting is used, ie fashion and home accessories, because in these areas, designs and patterns must both be effective in their own right and fit in with their surroundings. In fabric design there is a vast range of designs available for dresses, blouses, collars and cuffs and belts, as well as for shawls, cushions, scarves and curtains.

Crazy Patterns should be used only as a source of inspiration for arranging a variety of shapes decoratively. Transfer sketch (**1**); colour chart (**2**).

Crazy Patterns

This is a crazy fabric design put together using both bizarre and natural shapes. They are creatively linked by the basic yellow-green theme. The large leaves offer distinct focal points in what is otherwise a very complex pattern (**3**).

MATERIALS
Silk: 60 × 60 cm (24 × 24 in) crêpe de Chine
Colours: iron-fixable silk painting colours
Top row of colour chart: yellow, turquoise
Middle row of colour chart: turquoise green, carmine
Bottom row of colour chart: claret, black
Brushes: sable brushes nos 8 and 3
Outliner: colourless spirit-based outliner
Technique: outliner technique and watercolour technique

Draw the design on to the silk using colourless spirit-based outliner as per the transfer sketch, and leave it to dry.

Next, paint the individual shapes in the given colours.

Paint the background using the wet-on-wet technique in diluted shades of turquoise, yellow and claret. Leave to dry, steam fix and clean.

You could also paint the pattern in colours set on a black background, as in the Stars and Leaves design (see page 124).

1

2

3

COLOUR VARIATIONS

Leaf Mosaic

This design invites you to experiment with brushes and colours. You can paint the background mosaic as the mood takes you. An array of patterns is depicted on the transfer sketch and these are reproduced in picture 5. The playful charm of the mosaic is already detectable in the graphic draft (**1**).

Leaf on a Blue-green Mosaic

The mixed blue-green colours exude an exotic air. This is further emphasised by the violet shades (**2**).

Leaf on a Yellow-red Mosaic

This motif has a summer feel to it as a result of the many warm colour shades. This effect is strengthened by the contrasting blue shades (**3**).

Leaf on a Purple Mosaic

The black contours define the individual shapes giving the picture a stained glass effect. Thus, with just a few colours, you can create a strong impact (**5**).

MATERIALS
Silk: 30 × 24 cm (12 × 9½ in) crêpe de Chine
Colours: iron-fixable silk painting colours
Top row of colour chart: yellow, pink
Middle row of colour chart: turquoise, turquoise green
Bottom row of colour chart: blue, aubergine
Brushes: sable brushes nos 8 and 3
Outliner: black outliner
Technique: outliner technique and watercolour technique

Draw the design on to the silk using black outliner. In order to avoid smudging lines already drawn, start with the horizontal lines and allow them to dry. Then draw the vertical lines and leave these to dry. Next draw the leaf, and once it has dried, draw the rest of the design. The outliner must be thoroughly dry before you begin to paint.

Paint the design in the given colours. For the leaf itself mix a light, greenish yellow and add just the tiniest amount of blue to the yellow. Paint the leaf, using the wet-on-wet technique, in the greenish-yellow and the full-tone yellow. Leave to dry then fix using an iron.

This design is well suited to a great many colour variations. Indeed, it invites you to indulge in different colour combinations. The large leaf will always be clearly distinguishable from the small detail of the background. Therefore, paint the squares as the mood takes you. You could also use the salt technique on some of the mosaic shapes (see page 58) or the thinning technique (see page 70). Give your imagination free rein. This is the best and most visual way of getting to know a great many of the different effects of colour, structure and contrast.

1 Transfer sketch.

2 Blue, green and violet shades can be used to create an air of the exotic.

3 Warm red and yellow tones give added vibrancy.

4 Colour chart.

5 Black outlines create a stained glass effect.

1

2

3

4 and 5

OSCILLATIONS

1

2

Colours and shapes swing into one another in a gentle rhythm. The particular impact of this cheerful design stems from the contrast of warm and cold colour tones and from the playful alternation between restful colour areas and delicate colour runs.

MATERIALS

Silk: 17 × 35 cm (6½ × 14 in) crêpe de Chine
Colours: iron-fixable silk painting colours
Top row of colour chart: yellow, violet, turquoise, turquoise green
Bottom row of colour chart: pink, claret, ultramarine blue
Outliner: black outliner
Technique: outliner technique and watercolour technique

Draw the design using black outliner and leave to dry thoroughly (**1**).

Paint all the closed shapes in the given colours. Paint the yellow leaf shapes using the watercolour technique wet-on-wet. Make sure that you leave some white showing in the leaves (**2**).

Apply the colourful background within the border, also using the wet-on-wet technique. This is not particularly easy in this design because many different colours are drawn into each other. The recommended order in which to work is the following: mix all the colour tones that you will need for the background on a white porcelain plate. Then apply water to the background. Do not allow any pools of water to form. Paint on the damp surface using two brushes, one for the colours and one watercolour brush to blend together the colours. Firstly, paint the three open arcs in

bright pink, very bright violet and bright yellow. In each case draw the colour out from the middle of the arc to the left and to the right. However, paint up to just before the openings and not right to the end of each arc. As the intention is not to allow hard edges to form at the end of the arc, do not allow the colour to dry. Therefore, paint over the arc a second time using the watercolour brush.

Next, apply the green shades of turquoise green and a mixture of turquoise green and a little yellow to the background. A gentle run should be created at the beginning of each arc. Apply the warm violet and blue shades in the same way (**4**).

Now paint the outer border pale yellow. Fix (**5**).

Try out the following variations:

Textured oscillations
Alter the background by using the salt effect.

Gentle oscillations
Draw the design using silver outliner and paint the shapes using gently blending, pearly pastel shades.

Bold oscillations
Draw the design using colourless outliner. Close the open arcs using outliner. Paint the shapes in strong, bright colours. Paint the background within the border black. The black will increase the brilliance of your colours.

Graduated blue oscillations

Mix up an attractive blue in various bright shades using water. You could also mix it with a little red or green. Draw the design using black outliner and then paint the areas using the blue shades.

1 Draw the design on to the white silk using black spirit-based outliner.

2 Paint all the closed sections of the design.

3 Colour chart.

4 A black border increases the brilliance of the colours.

5 Apply the background in different colour shades using the watercolour technique, wet-on-wet.

4

5

FLOWERS

In silk painting, as in nature, it is colours that provide variety. Floral designs are very well suited to colour variations. Before you paint on the silk, try out various colours in sketches first (2, 3 and 4).

MATERIALS
Silk: 30 × 40 cm (12 × 16 in) habutai silk
Colours: iron-fixable silk painting colours
Top row of colour chart: yellow, turquoise
Middle row of colour chart: claret, aubergine

Bottom row of colour chart: may green, blue
Brush: no 8 sable brush
Outliner: colourless outliner
Hair dryer
Technique: outliner technique and watercolour technique

Draw the design using colourless outliner and leave to dry.

Before you begin painting, mix up the following colour shades: a bright, a medium and an orange yellow and various green shades made from blue, may green and yellow for the plant; aubergine,

made from a little claret for part of the background and the stamen and the blue shades with may green for rest of the background. Using the wet-on-wet technique, paint the flower. Leave some light patches. Allow to dry.

Wash out the three lower petals so that dark colour edges form in the calyx. Fix the painting using the hair dryer. If the edges do not become dark enough, draw in a little orange and dry it using the hair dryer. If necessary, repeat the wash-out procedure.

Then, wet-on-wet, paint the remaining part of the plant. Leave some light patches on the large leaf. Using a dry brush paint the stamen and dry with the hair dryer. Paint the background wet-on-wet so that an iridescent effect is created. If this proves too difficult, paint the background using just one colour. Leave to dry and then fix.

1 Transfer sketch.
2 Red colour sketch.
3 Yellow colour sketch.
4 Blue colour sketch.
5 Colour chart.
6 Yellow Flower.

1

2

3

4

5

GLOSSARY

Complementary colours: the complementary colours are red and green, yellow and violet, and blue and orange. They lie opposite each other respectively on the colour wheel. If complementary colours are mixed together a grey colour shade is created.

Edges: edges are created if you paint damp colours on to dry colours or dry silk. Therefore, in order to avoid unwanted edges, both the colours and the silk must be wet when painting. Edges are also formed when washing out.

Effect salt: special large-grain salt used for the salt technique.

Fixing: fixing makes the silk painting colourfast and prevents the colours from running when the silk is washed. Traditional silk painting colours are fixed using steam; iron-fixable colours are fixed using an iron; liquid-fixable colours are fixed using a chemical solution. Before fixing, a mere drop of water can ruin an entire silk painting.

Flow properties: the flow properties of silk painting colours are influenced by the type of silk used and its degree of dampness. Colours flow more quickly on thin material than they do on thicker silks. Even the direction of the silk's warp and weft yarns can influence the flow properties. Thinning increases colour flow. Colours flow better on damp silk than they do on dry silk. Primers restrict colour flow.

Iron fixing: iron-fixable colours are fixed using an electric iron. After drying, the reverse side of the silk is ironed for four to five minutes, depending on the product.

Liquid fixing: the colours are fixed by applying a chemical substance that must later be washed off.

Masked (or reserved) areas: this term is given to areas treated with outliner. Here no more colour can penetrate the silk. If the area that has already been painted has outliner applied to it, the colour on to which the outliner is applied will remain as it is, even if it is overpainted.

Mix-white: a 'mix-white' is available for lightening certain iron-fixable colours. It does not have the transparency of the usual silk painting colours.

Outliner: a resist agent through which no colour can penetrate. Most outliner is water-based, although spirit-based outliners are also available. Originally gutta – a rubber-based resist agent was used; it can still be bought but is not common. Outliners (both types) are often referred to as gutta, even though they are not.

Outliner lines also called gutta outlines: this is the name given to the lines treated with outliner. Here no more colour can penetrate the silk. If an area that has already been painted has outliner applied to it, the colour on to which the outliner is applied will remain as it is, even if it is overpainted.

Overlaying technique: using traditional silk painting colours you can overpaint in several layers. If, however, certain areas or lines have been masked using spirit-based outliner the colours beneath the outliner retained, even if they are overpainted. You can also create coloured and hidden outliner lines in this way.

Perspective: dark, strong and warm colours force their way through, visually, into the foreground. Pale, light and cold colours appear more distant. This effect is called atmospheric perspective.

Primary colours: the primary colours are red, yellow and blue. All other colours (secondary colours and mixed colour shades) are mixed from these three primary colours.

Primer: colour flow is lessened considerably by primers. Therefore, it is easy to paint contour lines on silk to which a primer has been applied without having to use outliner lines. The two primers are gutta petrol primer and salt primer. Ready-mixed primers are available commercially.

Salt technique: salt grains are laid on to damp silk. Flower- and ray-like structures form, and the salt can break down some mixed colours into their original component colours.

Outliner technique: the purpose of outliners is to stop the flow of colours on the silk. Outliners are used to apply clear dividing lines and to cover areas into which no more colour should penetrate. Spirit-based outliner or gutta is used with traditional silk painting colours and is thinned using Essence F; water-soluble

outliner is used with iron-fixable colours. Both coloured and colourless outliners are available. Lines and smaller areas can be painted in colour using coloured outliners for iron-fixable and traditional silk painting colours. Coloured outliners are opaque. Most work is carried out using colourless outliners. After painting, those lines or areas that were covered with outliner appear in their original colour.

Steam fixing: the traditional silk painting colours are fixed using steam. To do this, use a pressure cooker or a special steamer. Enquire whether anyone offers a specialist steam fixing service in your area.

Thinner: traditional silk painting colours are thinned using either a commercially available thinner (sometimes called a dilutant), a mixture of water and alcohol. The greater the proportion of water, the slower the colours dry. This is important if you are painting wet-on-wet. Iron-fixable colours are thinned using water only.

Three-dimensional effect: by applying slightly darkened shading to those areas of the image which, within the context of the picture, are out of the light, you can create a three-dimensional effect.

Transfer sketch: these sketches include all contours and all outliner lines. Even at the transfer sketch stage make sure that all shapes are properly sealed so that no colour can escape.

Wash-out technique: after drying, silk painting colours can be washed out. For traditional colours use thinner; for iron-fixable colours use water. Both loosen the colours and force them to spread.

Watercolour technique: colours are painted on damp silk, wet-on-wet, into one another. This results in very attractive colour runs. The watercolour technique is very suitable for combining with the outliner technique.

Water marks: see **Edges**

Wet-on-wet technique: the colours are painted on to silk dampened with water. This can give rise to very attractive merging colour flows.

BIBLIOGRAPHY

Campbell-Harding, Valerie
Fabric Painting for Embroidery
(Batsford, 1991)

Dawson, Pam
How to Paint on Silk
(Search Press, 1988)

Dawson, Pam
The Art of Painting on Silk
4 vols, Search Press, 1987–1990)

Hahn, Susanne
A Complete Guide to Silk Painting
(Search Press, 1992)

Henge, Renate
Inspirational Silk Painting from Nature
(Search Press, 1990)

Kennedy, Jill and Varrall, Jane
Painting on Silk
(Batsford, 1988)

Kennedy, Jill and Varrall, Jane
Silk Painting: Techniques and Ideas
(Batsford, 1991)

Ottelart, Lydie
Painting Flowers on Silk
(Search Press, 1991)

SILK PAINTING MATERIALS' SUPPLIERS

United Kingdom

Atlantis Art Materials
2 St Andrews Way
London
E3 3PA
Tel: 071-537 2727

Wm H Bennett & Sons Ltd
Crown Royal Park
Higher Hillgate
Stockport
SK1 3HB
Tel: 061-477 5979
(Silk merchants)

Candle Makers' Suppliers
28 Blythe Road
London
W14 OHA
Tel: 071-602 4031

L. Cornelissen & Son Ltd
105 Great Russell Street
London WC1B 3RY
Tel: 071-636 1045

Craft Creations Ltd
Unit 1-7
Harpers Yard
Ruskin Road
London N17 8NE
Tel: 081-885 2655

Cromartie Hobbycraft Ltd
Park Hall Road
Longton
Stoke on Trent
ST3 5AY
Tel: 0782 319435

Frisk Products Ltd
7-11 Franthorne Way
Randlesdown Road
London SE6 3BT
Tel: 081-698 3481
(Distributors for Artograph)

Green and Stone
259 Kings Road
London SW3 5EL
Tel: 071-352 6521 or 0837

Pongees Ltd
184-186 Old Street
London EC1V 9FR
Tel: 071-253 0428
Silk merchants

Panduro Hobby Ltd
Westway House
Transport Avenue
Brentford
Middlesex
Tel: 081-847 6161

Painting on Silk (mail order)
22 Wainwright Road
Altrincham
Cheshire
WA14 4BW

George Weil & Sons Ltd
Shop:
18 Hanson Street
London W1P 7DB
Tel: 071-580 3763

Mail order (worldwide):
The Warehouse
Reading Arch Road
Redhill
Surrey RH1 1HG
Tel: 0737 778868

Australia, New Zealand, South Africa

Arts and Crafts Depot,
40 Harrison Street
Johannesburg
South Africa

Batik Oetoro
203 Avoca Street
Randwick NSW 2031
Tel: (12) 398 6201

Francheville (Aust) Pty Ltd
1-5 Perry Street (P.O. Box 1591)
Collingwood VIC 3066
Tel: (03) 416 0611
(Wholesalers)

Marie France
92 Currie Street
Adelaide SA 5000
Tel: (08) 51 4138

Silk Road
P.O. Box 2422
Gosford NSW 2250
Tel: (043) 67 6449

R.G Elsegood (Sales) Pty Ltd
Silk House
8 Little Queen Street
Chippendale NSW 2008
Tel: (02) 319 2266
(Silk merchants)

J. and C. Agencies
P.O. Box 278
Sans Souci NSW 2219
Tel: (02) 529 3615

Silk Fabrics
127 Pilkinston Road
Panmure
Auckland
Tel (09) 570 4366

Rainbow Screen Printers
5b Ashfield Street
Gelnfield
Tel: (09) 444 7790

Barbara von Seida
Waiuna Bay Road
Coromandel
Tel: (07) 866 8452

INDEX